Curriculum Development

Curriculum Development

G. ROBERT KOOPMAN

42041

The Center for Applied Research in Education, Inc.

New York

Foreword

An ever increasing number of school systems regard curriculum development as an integral part of their educational responsibilities. Most schools have moved away from the "expert" approach, where one person or only a few people were consulted in an attempt to improve the curriculum. They have moved toward the "cooperative" method wherein many faculty members and consultants are involved in this task. Today more people are involved in curriculum development than at any time in the history of education. Without question this is a sound and productive practice if the people involved are properly informed regarding background, content, and methodology. If they are not, the process of curriculum development can be confusing, frustrating, and unproductive. This has happened in many cases.

Many books, research studies, and articles have been written on improving the curriculum. This volume *Curriculum Development* should be of value to the curriculum worker because of its unique features. For example, in a relatively few pages, this publication describes the early beginnings of curriculum development and the effects of the great depression; it brings out more recent developments and explains what basic concepts should be considered in curriculum development. The relationship of curriculum development to in-service education is discussed along with ideas on organization, new practices, the great issues, and the challenges future curriculum development will have to meet.

The content of this volume is based on statements of outstanding authorities as well as on experiences of many school systems. Dr. Koopman is well qualified to write on this subject because of his varied and practical background. In addition to his extensive writing and editing experiences, he has spent a lifetime in educational administration, research, teaching, and curriculum development—all with an emphasis on research and development. He has directed or been a consultant on curriculum development in many local communities, in many states as well as in India, Germany, and Italy—the latter group under the auspices of the United States Army and the United States Foreign Service. Many of his generalizations grew out of his experiences with the Michigan Curriculum Program.

Curriculum Development should be on the "required" reading list of all people who are directly involved or merely interested in how to move our curriculum forward to meet the challenging demands of today's and tomorrow's world.

THERAL T. HERRICK
Executive Director, Michigan
Council on Economic Education
Professor of Economic Education
University of Michigan

Curriculum Development

G. Robert Koopman

One of the fundamental activities of teachers and administrators is curriculum development. Its importance to education is obvious, yet there have been few attempts in the literature to analyze curriculum development as an educational movement. G. Robert Koopman has written a significant book in which he both analyzes curriculum development as an educational movement and predicts what the future development might be as a result of the influences of modern forces.

Dr. Koopman discusses the antecedents and early beginnings of curriculum development both as a scholar and as a person who participated as a leader in the movement. In fact, one of the most interesting aspects of this volume is that to a considerable extent it is autobiographical.

Factors influencing curriculum development are analyzed from the depression period of the 1930's to recent space age innovations. After having presented the background, the author moves into the descriptive aspects of the movement: basic concepts, organization for curriculum development, in-service education as an end-product of curriculum development, and new practices. The book concludes with a presentation of the major issues still unresolved and with outlooks for future curriculum development.

G. Robert Koopman has long been a leader in education. He has written widely and has held many responsible positions. Prior to his retirement, he was a top administrator in the Michigan State Education Department.

DANIEL E. GRIFFITHS
Content Editor

Contents

CHAPTER I

Antecedents and Early Beginnings of Curriculum Development

Until the time of the pronounced social and industrial revolutions of the early twentieth century, curriculums were thought of and written of as fairly static solutions to the needs of social systems. Since the social systems were subject to relatively slow social change the curriculum could be worked out as a definite solution to the educational problem of a given society. The concept of curriculum as a constant and perfectible instrument was accepted and acceptable. Status rather than change dominated educational philosophy and practice.

The revolutionary changes that took place in the first half of the twentieth century were so violent and sudden that they changed not only methods of producing goods but also basic social institutions and processes. In the field of education they even gave birth to new processes such as educational research and curriculum development. These processes are easily understood when the relatively static societies of the nineteenth century and twentieth century cultures that have not yet been swept into the rapid current of social change are contrasted with those that are already engulfed.

Educational change is, of course, a constant in societies in the sense that form and content are continually changing to some extent. But prior to World War I change was a negligible factor. Educational leadership was then concerned primarily with the establishment of schools and school systems, with the extension of philosophical thinking, with the regularization of existing curriculums and with the perfection and spread of traditional practices of teaching. There had been a few attempts to broaden the curriculum by bringing in physical education and industrial arts but by and large the elementary school curriculum was quite standardized and the secondary school curriculum equally so.

The twentieth century with its turbulent changes in industrialized countries seriously challenged the validity of the school curriculum. The usefulness of the traditional elementary school curriculum which was based on the simplest elements of moral training and literacy skills began to be questioned by many people. Even more vigorously was the college-preparatory curriculum of the secondary schools criticized.

Experimental psychology and educational philosophy were developing rapidly in the early decades of the twentieth century. Their development had a definite impact on the processes that went on in the school and the classroom as well as on educational objectives and curriculum patterns.

The result of these developments was the widespread modernization of curriculums that began about 1920 and led to the development of a rational, educational planning process which has come to be called *curriculum development*.

This volume is concerned primarily and basically with the history and establishment of that process and with the principles, practices and problems of curriculum development.

The antecedents of curriculum development reach back into philosophy, history of social thought and history of education. Actually, however, curriculum development is a twentieth century phenomenon. Its beginnings follow closely on the beginnings of the professionalization of teaching. In point of time it can be said that deliberate and systematic *curriculum revision* first occurred after World War I and that *curriculum development* as a well-defined and technical process appeared about a decade later. Thus, some educators in service in 1960 have lived through the entire period of this development.

The Importance of Curriculum Decisions

The education of its young has been a matter of great concern to peoples in all cultures at all times. Anthropological and historical studies reveal how educational programs have developed and how they have functioned in various cultures from primitive to modern times. Curriculum decisions were often made with little or no consciousness on the part of the decision makers. Parents, philosophers, priests, chiefs and tradesmen helped make the decisions. It was after the rise of nationalism that national governments became directly concerned with decision making. Political leaders, chiefs of state and ministers of the government made decisions by issuing fiats and by appropriating resources for education. Legislatures issued broad authorizations. Curriculum mandates such as the Northwest Ordinance of 1787 of the United States Congress directed that education be encouraged and it made valuable resources available.

The *Encyclopedia of Educational Research* points out that:

> Traditionally, the main directions in curriculum development were determined by textbook authors and by administrators. The curriculum resources were the textbook and the teacher. There were, of course, many others, but they were not taken into account in any constructive way by those who planned or formulated curriculums and instructional policies. As the conception of curriculum and of the objectives of education broadened, the need for different types of resources arose. Those who prepare resource materials today try to provide material concerning the problems about which learners may need assistance. These are the current problems that students are becoming concerned about now at their various present ages and stages of development. Good curriculum resource materials are designed to stimulate the development of desirable attitudes, efficient work habits, open-minded approaches to controversial questions, scientific attitudes toward the solution of problems, broad appreciation of the arts, and all the other objectives of modern education. In a sense, curriculum resources are as wide as living itself.
>
> It follows from all of this that the processes of curriculum planning have changed greatly and, if trends continue, will change still more. In the early history of education, the curriculum was a social and intellectual bank in which was deposited the accumulated wisdom of a people to be drawn upon as needed by its youth. At present the trend is definitely toward a flexible curriculum, where the planning is done primarily in terms of the developing needs and abilities of the learners against the background of the needs of society, the relative usefulness of various knowledges and skills, and the logical and psychological nature of learning.[1]

The making of decisions concerning curriculum policy, however, is not what is meant by curriculum development. Nor is curriculum revision the same thing. Prior to World War I American teachers and administrators were not particularly conscious of curriculum problems, since the curriculum did not seem to change much. Only a very few people realized that the curriculum of the secondary school had not adjusted to meet the needs of the industrial revolution. Fewer still realized that the educational method was based largely upon tacit assumptions rather than upon research and experimentation. The philosophical thinking and experimentation of John Dewey and Francis Parker had virtually no impact on normative practice. Very few professional courses dealt critically

---

[1] Chester W. Harris, ed., *Encyclopedia of Educational Research*, 3rd ed. (New York: The Macmillan Co., 1960), p. 361.

with the problem of learning. The research and thinking of E. L. Thorndike was known at the time to only a few people.

Teachers were expected to teach the courses of study as they existed in syllabi and textbooks. Change was not generally recognized. There was so little recognition of change that improved student performance loomed above curriculum change in the minds of all but a few people whose voices were scarcely heard. Normal schools were set up for teachers where they could learn to teach the common curriculum in a "normal" or acceptable manner. In days when professional teachers in the modern sense didn't exist and when mass education was just coming into existence, standardization of the utilization of "best practice" in the graded school was very important.

The Cracks in the Facade

Increased affluence, new inventions, changes in social thought and the first world war in history greatly increased perceptions of people both in and out of the field of education to the need for revising the curriculum. What Rousseau had guessed about the social personality and its relation to society became more obvious. What Pestalozzi divined about the affective life of the child was translated into a new way of teaching. Further, industrial society changed the life of the child and demanded a different kind of educated person than had been required previously.

The usefulness of the selective secondary school with its narrow and rigid curriculum was questioned in a burgeoning society based on a democratic philosophy.

The early antecedents of curriculum development were evident in the second decade of the new century. It was the decade 1920–1930, however, that saw the flowering of curriculum revision and curriculum construction which contained the seeds of a new and more complete process called *curriculum development*. The gradual acceptance of curriculum development as a process and as an essential aspect of teaching and administration came later.

Curriculum Revision as Transition

The emergence and nature of curriculum development can best be understood by examining its relationship to curriculum revision. Curriculum revision consisted essentially of three processes: (1) revaluing and reconsidering the curriculum in the light of changed conditions in society, (2) reorganizing the curriculum in terms of new educational knowledge of a technical nature—such as findings about the psychology of learning, and (3) revising courses of study based on both newer social conditions and changing technical knowledge concerning education.

This process of revision was so important that it is considered as one of the principal forces in the professionalization of education. Those educators who were pressing for educational reform found a road to progress. Suddenly the newer findings in the psychology of learning became significant to educational leaders and teachers. Educational researchers found many tasks in the curriculum field and found that their findings were appreciated. The problem of educational method took on new proportions. Educational sociology which was in its earliest stage attracted the attention of educators. It enhanced curriculum revision and, in turn, was greatly enhanced by it. The breakthrough of vocational education was facilitated by the curriculum revision movement in the years immediately succeeding World War I.

Curriculum revision laid the foundation for curriculum development because it dealt, in a limited way, with the fundamental problems of education that curriculum development was to deal with more thoroughly, efficiently and continuously. The fundamental problem areas were the following:

1. The role of the school in society;
2. The objectives of education;
3. The selection of effective learning experiences related to chosen objectives;
4. The organization of learning experiences into a total curriculum and into teaching-learning procedures;
5. The evaluation of the curriculum and of teaching methods; and
6. Cooperation in curriculum improvement.

The Cardinal Principles of Secondary Education[2] which represent a breakthrough in secondary education illustrate the way in which these major problems were approached. The effort in this field started an attack aimed at the improvement of secondary education that still goes on. Brilliant figures such as Inglis and Briggs emerged. Powerful forces such as those behind vocational education became activated and organized. Research was initiated, energized and directed.

---

[2] N.E.A., Commission on the Reorganization of Secondary Education, *Cardinal Principles of Secondary Education*—U.S. Bureau of Education Bulletin 1918, No. 35 (Washington, D.C.: Government Printing Office, 1918).

Curriculum revision represented a revolution in educational practice and coincided with some revolutionary social changes such as the application of democratic processes in everyday life. It also provided the requisite midwifery for the curriculum development movement.

The Rise of Curriculum Development

Reference has been made to the contributions made by curriculum revision but it was its own weaknesses that brought about its demise. Once educators started to question curriculum and educational practice they refused to stop with revisionism. Long before the great economic depression shook the foundations of the curriculum, leading educators began to reject revisionism. The need for a better approach was gradually recognized.

And so the process of curriculum development grew out of the beginnings of early curriculum thinking and more especially out of curriculum revision. Good examples of curriculum development began to appear between 1925–1930 and these were generally accepted, if not widely practiced, in local school districts and in state school systems around 1930. State programs of curriculum development became quite common during the decade 1930–1940 when Virginia, California, Florida, Illinois, Michigan and Wisconsin demonstrated significant approaches and programs.

The Nature of Curriculum and Curriculum Development

Any discussion of curriculum development must take into account varying concepts and definitions of "curriculum." Traditionally, a curriculum was a collection of syllabuses and textbooks in a given school or class of schools. In some schools and cultures this definition is still correct. As the purposes of education have broadened and as educators have become more understanding of educational problems and processes, the concept of curriculum has changed. Edward A. Krug refers to the curriculum as "all the means employed by the school to provide students with opportunities for desirable learning experiences."[3] This definition varies little from many others in current use. Contrasted with the traditional concept, however, such a definition tremendously affected the philosophy, objectives, content, method and evaluation of the current curriculum. All these

---

[3] Edward A. Krug, *Administering Curriculum Planning* (New York: Harper & Row, Publishers, 1956), p. 4.

assumed new proportions and relationships. Even so, the definition did not have enough latitude to accommodate some of the newer developments—such as the community school development. The emphasis on "employed by the school" seemed to ignore learnings achieved by chance or design outside of the school. But the definition was and still remains fairly functional and satisfactory to the profession.

Two references show the great breadth of the new concept of curriculum. Both of the references that follow are rather basic and extreme. Hence they tend to define the limits of the concept rather than the heart of it.

The concept of contributory education. Bobbitt[4] used the term "basic education" to refer to the out-of-school learning experiences of the child which he assumed to be essentially the responsibility of the family. He gave to the school the secondary but nevertheless important responsibility of providing "contributory education":

> ... such as the following: (1) to look seriously and responsibly at the nature, situation, and educational needs of every child in every family that it serves; (2) to discover how each child and youth carries on his twenty-four-hour continuity of activities; (3) to discover how each ought to carry them on under the conditions; (4) to note the ways and degrees in which each falls short of what he ought to be doing; (5) to note the kinds of enlightenment, conditioning, stimulation, and guidance required for preventing or remedying the deficiencies; (6) to plan its program of exercises day after day as carefully as a physician plans the treatment of his individual patients, so as properly to influence the twenty-four-hour living of each child and youth; (7) to help the pupils know with reasonable certainty and clearness what they ought daily to be thinking and doing in their self-planning and self-guidance; (8) to make the life at school for several hours each school day a carefully conditioned and supervised segment of wholesome living; (9) to provide clear, concrete patterns of all kinds of desirable behavior; (10) to help the pupils to the knowledge needed for valuations and self-direction; (11) to help them to the skills required for facility of execution; (12) to stimulate and to reinforce the wills of the children and youths where such reinforcement is necessary; (13) to shape the valuations, attitudes, and emotional gradients of the children and youths in such a way as to predispose them to the behavior sanctioned by understanding; (14) to help the parents understand matters well enough to carry on their share of the work; (15) to provide

---

4 Franklin Bobbitt, *The Curriculum of Modern Education* (New York: McGraw-Hill Book Co., © 1941), pp. 23–24. Used by permission.

the professional leadership and to cooperate with the families in the guidance and supervision of the young people; and (16) to help everybody understand how well they are doing their several portions, and to perceive the character of the life that each child and youth is achieving.

In general, schools in free, industrialized societies have tended to assume the functions proposed by Bobbitt even though they have put tremendous responsibilities on the schools.

The community school concept. The community school concept extended educational planning and institutional responsibilities even further. Earlier statements of purposes, objectives and responsibilities focussed primarily on the individual. The community as the situation in which education, and particularly social education, takes place gradually received more emphasis. The curriculum of learners, both young and old, was defined by the author as "the learner's environment in motion."[5] This definition is designed to make a point. It plays down the importance of the teacher dominating a classroom group and plays up the learner's readiness, initiative, perception and actual experiences. It also allows an adequate role for the educational importance of the total environment including the family, the community and the mass media. It allows for a full-scale guidance program. In *My Town* the curriculum is described as a cultural instrument:

> The community school concept contributes materially to a novel solution to the community problem. But it alone is insufficient. To simply readjust the school program would be to ignore the greater principle, namely, that community living is the source of values and of learning. No one institution or approach can care for all of the learning needs of the people. It is necessary to invent a new concept—one that has been missing in previous formulations of the solution. *This is the concept of the community curriculum or the sum total of all of the planned and contrived learning experiences of the community, of the impact of all of the natural and man-made resources of the community, of all of the supervised education, recreation, and group work in the community.* It refers to all of the creative learning experiences of the people of a community. It is a community curriculum in the sense that it grows out of the needs, interests, resources and conditions of the community. It is a curriculum, thus it is *planned* within minimal limits. It is planned and thus

---

[5] G. Robert Koopman, *My Town—Planning the American Community and Its School—Toward a Twentieth Century Solution* (The Author—out of print, 1956), p. 2.

it requires a marshalling of resources and facilities, each one in relation to the other.[6]

None of these emphases or developments negates the definition cited earlier but it must be understood that *curriculum development* takes place in the field of curriculum and is profoundly affected by new developments in that field. It should be noted also that these formulations of purpose and direction were rather theoretical. Yet they were necessary to round out the development of public education in a free, open society. Nowhere have schools perfected the program planning and carried out the functions specified.

Curriculum Development Defined

Curriculum development is that aspect of teaching and administration that designedly, systematically, cooperatively and continuously seeks to improve the teaching-learning process. This definition can be applied to the professional teacher and his own responsibilities, to a school or to any complex of schools or school systems. Curriculum development can be a part of teaching or a part of administration or both. It can be partial, broken-front or uniform in nature. It is nearly always present where teaching is going on. Curriculum development should not be confused with curriculum change since curriculum change takes place inexorably with or without curriculum development—yet curriculum change is an inevitable result of curriculum development.

The ultimate criterion. The ultimate evaluative criterion of curriculum development is more and better learning—more learning with a given amount of effort and cost—better learning in the sense that negative concomitants are held to the minimum; and better learning in terms of the wise selection of objectives and emphases.

The choice of terms in the curriculum improvement field is illuminating. Somewhat in order there appeared curriculum revision, curriculum construction, curriculum building, curriculum improvement, program improvement, curriculum planning and curriculum development. The term "reorganizing" appeared and still appears, but not to indicate the name of the general process. All of these terms were and are descriptive of the activities to which they were applied. The term *curriculum development*, however, has gained acceptance because it is broad enough to embrace many of the earlier concepts

---

[6] *Ibid.,* p. 9.

and is suggestive of the many processes involved. It is embodied in the rather odd names of the principal national and state organizations that give leadership in the specialized field, such as the Association for Supervision and Curriculum Development and its affiliates.

Defining the process of curriculum development as that aspect of teaching and administration that designedly, systematically, cooperatively and continuously seeks to improve the teaching-learning process agrees with the authoritative literature of education. It does extend the definition beyond that in the *Dictionary of Education:* "a systematic procedure of developing a suitable curriculum for a particular school or school system. . . ."[7] This definition fails to include the idea of continuity of process and also fails to include the phenomenon of the professional teacher or tutor who assiduously experiments and records, or remembers, in order to improve the teaching-learning processes for which he is responsible. Indeed, many such teachers "report" their tested procedures and thus help the profession to improve. Such a report is well illustrated in the book *Teacher-Pupil Planning.*[8]

The Philosophers and the Commissions

The philosophers. Prior to 1920 such curriculum change as there was in the United States was influenced substantially by the thinking of a few men of great authority and prestige, and by the reports of commissions. Commission reports reflected the opinions of the educational philosophers. Since educational research was practically non-existent, authority, tradition and philosophy as expressed by these men were very influential.

John Dewey and William Heard Kilpatrick were especially effective in bringing about changes in curriculum and method. Dewey, as the leading exponent of the philosophy of instrumentalism, spelled out the implications of that philosophy for education. He stressed the need of the individual for education, the importance of experience to learning, the relation of the learner to society, the relation of the school to society, and the implications of democracy to education in all of its phases.

---

[7] Carter V. Good, ed., *Dictionary of Education,* rev. ed. (New York: McGraw-Hill Book Co., 1959).

[8] Louise Parrish and Yvonne Waskin, *Teacher-Pupil Planning—For Better Curriculum Learning* (New York: Harper & Row, Publishers, 1958).

Kilpatrick, an able educational philosopher himself, became the great teacher of teachers. He based his work squarely on the philosophy of instrumentalism and worked out the implications in the fields of method, curriculum and personal behavior. The concept of an individual continuously changed by experience versus the idea of adding knowledges and skills at will to an individual had a powerful impact on education and a peculiar and forceful impact on curriculum theory and practice.

The professionalization of teaching and the elevation of education to the graduate level occurring at about the same time contributed to the emergence of strong personalities in all fields of education. Thorndike, Bode, Courtis, Charters, Bobbitt, Cubberley, Bonser, Judd and Bagley were outstanding leaders who greatly influenced developments in education.

Edward L. Thorndike had a unique effect on teaching and curriculum development since he dealt directly with learning in a new manner. Using the experimental approach he called attention to the nature of learning and its role in human behavior. His influence reached across the land and revolutionized teacher education. Educational practices, curriculum content and curriculum organization were all brought under critical scrutiny. This development created a favorable role for curriculum development and helped start the educational research movement.

Early commissions and committees. Early commissions and committees influenced curriculum decisions very decidedly between 1890 and 1920. As the need for curriculum change became more apparent various commissions were appointed to make recommendations. The most famous of these was the Committee of Ten which sought to bring order and quality to secondary education. Its reports had great impact on the nature of secondary education during the early decades of the twentieth century and created a standardized "high school curriculum" in the United States.

The Commission on the Reorganization of Secondary Education[9] reporting in 1918 sought to broaden the scope of secondary education. This report, reflecting as it did the impact of the social revolution, put so many new obligations on the secondary school that its role was to be changed. While the changes were not made at once the report set forth a challenge and a task that greatly enriched and

---

[9] N.E.A., Commission on the Reorganization of Secondary Education, *Cardinal Principles of Secondary Education*—U.S. Bureau of Education Bulletin 1918, No. 35 (Washington, D.C.: Government Printing Office, 1918).

guided curriculum development work at the secondary school level. The theorists and the secondary school principals as a group continued to explore the meanings and directions of this report until such time as newer reports which embodied much of the earlier one attracted their attention. Among other effects, this commission report laid a basis for vocational education which was to sweep the country during the ensuing decade.

These early commission reports established a pattern of action for educators which is still followed although research findings tend to gradually supplant authority.

The Influence of Administrative Theory

While the curriculum development movement grew largely out of cultural needs and the psychological needs of a developing education profession, it was influenced by administrative theory. Cubberley, Strayer and Engelhart using an empirical approach stressed administrative responsibilities in the field of instruction. Moehlman gave instructional leadership the central role in his functional theory of administration. Dewey's emphasis on making the school experience an experience in democratic living laid the basis for democratic administration in the field of education. Experiments in democratic administration were tied up closely with curriculum development. It can be said that democratic administration and curriculum development in which cooperation, experimentation and process outweighed product developed together. These relationships were pointed out in one of the earliest books on democratic educational administration published in 1943.[10]

The Influence of Educational Research and Experimentation

Educational research which grew out of the newer developments in psychology came into being simultaneously with curriculum development and was a necessary companion. Educational experimmentation and educational testing were also parts of the new pattern of educational practice and leadership which was emerging.

The effects of these aspects of leadership were magnified by a new ferment in education based directly on the social revolution signalled

---

[10] G. Robert Koopman, Paul J. Misner and Alice M. Miel, *Democracy in School Administration* (New York: Appleton-Century-Crofts, Inc., 1943).

in by World War I. The Progressive Education Association was much more than a small educational association of laymen and professionals who wanted a better educational service. The PEA was a direct result of social ferment. It was a consumer of new ideas as well as a social force pushing schools toward revisionism and improvement. With the backing of the General Education Board and other foundations it sponsored research studies which served to promote curriculum development. The most notable of these was the Eight Year Study which did much to promote evaluation, critical analyses of college admission practices and curriculum development at the secondary school level.

The PEA combined a value emphasis such as child-centeredness with an emphasis on objectivity such as research, and these emphases had a double impact. The new tools of educational testing and educational research were put seriously to work.

The American Educational Research Association. The American Educational Research Association brought together people interested in educational research and publicized their work. Many of their early studies dealing with problems in the field of learning and curriculum were widely used by curriculum workers. Without educational research, curriculum studies could hardly have started.

The rapid development of professional education for teachers, for educational specialists and for administrators helped hasten the maturation of a process that came to be called curriculum development. The fundamental challenges of Kilpatrick, the analytical thinking of David Snedden in educational sociology, the emphatic approaches of Bagley and Judd, the objective approaches of Bobbitt and Charters were all disseminated through the new schools of education, mostly at the graduate level.

Curriculum Development as a Process

By the end of the third decade of the twentieth century the American culture had experienced a social revolution, a world war, a period of "normalcy," a temporary affluence, and an economic collapse. Fortunately, schools had become more viable as cultural establishments. Good schools in those days—and they were the better, not the norm of the profession—were administered by professional educational administrators bearing considerable responsibility. These schools tried their best to get professional teachers. Policy-making boards recognized educational research and they expected to be governed by it to some extent. These boards, like their administrators, dealt in ideas as well as management. They obligated their teachers to keep up-to-date and to help update the curriculum. They listened to parents and citizens even though they did not "involve" them. All concerned knew that certain school systems had re-thought their curriculums and instituted programs which kept their staffs alert and up-to-date.

In summation, it can be said that by 1930 the essential concept of curriculum development had not only emerged but had been tested and applied rather widely. Earlier concepts such as curriculum construction, curriculum revision, and reorganization of the curriculum had definitely proved to be inadequate. Curriculum development began to be conceived as commodious enough to embrace an entire set of activities: classroom experimentation, research studies, application of research studies, cooperative effort of a democratic nature, administrative leadership, and in-service education of staff members.

This was the situation when economic disaster struck the country.

CHAPTER II

Effects of the Great Depression
on Curriculum Development

The curriculum was both hindered and helped by the economic depression of the 1930's. Educational institutions suffered crippling budget reductions. Materials and manpower devoted to educational improvement were greatly reduced. These restrictions coupled with reduced incomes of educational personnel brought about serious staff demoralization. Still there was no shortage of ideas. Creative educators accepted the challenge of the times and recommended that new educational programs be designed to meet the needs of the new social situation. Many laymen felt the need for better educational programs. As a result, those educators seeking to improve educational programs found considerable support. Riding the wave of curriculum reform, creative administrators and curriculum specialists did exceedingly well in promoting experimentation and in improving curriculums.

The Effects on Education

The depression affected education in many ways. For the purposes of this discussion the principal effects, other than retrenchment, were as follows:

1. Education was subjected to severe criticism;
2. Educational research and experimentation were encouraged;
3. Education expanded into new areas;
4. Democratic principles and practices were applied to education;
5. Curriculum programs were expanded and strengthened; and
6. The roles of those concerned with curriculum development were re-oriented and clarified.

A brief discussion of each of these effects will indicate the sweep and importance of these developments.

Critcisms of education. Individuals and organizations charged with responsibility for education were aroused by the dilemma of education. A retrenchment in educational programs, occurring at a time when expansion and improvement were obviously needed, was criticised by many parents and citizens. Individuals outside of the field of education demanded more and better educational activity. Existing educational organizations proceeded to criticise education and make new proposals.

The National Education Association and the American Association of School Administrators established a new institution, the Educational Policies Commission. This Commission set up task forces which reviewed the educational status and issued a series of positive and clarifying reports such as *The Purposes of Education in American Democracy*.[1] All major state and national associations representing the education profession, including those specialized organizations affiliated with the National Education Association, issued new recommendations in their fields of special interest.

The American Youth Commission was created with foundation support to study the problems of American youth and to recommend remedies for youth problems.[2] Its work was ably supported and extended by the Educational Policies Commission which presented the volume *Education For All American Youth*.[3] The National Association of Secondary School Principals used its organizational resources to improve and broaden secondary school programs. The Regents' Inquiry in New York represented an exhaustive study of education in one state.

Two new educational societies organized. The Great Depression saw the birth of two new educational societies concerned primarily with curriculum development. The John Dewey Society, committed as it was to the philosophy of instrumentalism, brought out a series of yearbooks which spelled out the implications of that philosophy and the current social changes to education. These yearbooks were critical of normative practice in education and made rather basic suggestions for change. *Democracy and the Curriculum* dealt specifically with the curriculum problem.[4]

The Society for Curriculum Study was organized to study the technical field of curriculum development and its broader implications.

---

[1] Educational Policies Commission, *The Purpose of Education in American Democracy* (Washington, D.C.: National Education Association, 1938).

[2] American Youth Commission, *Youth and the Future* (Washington, D.C.: American Council on Education, 1942).

[3] Educational Policies Commission, *Education For All American Youth: A Further Look* (Washington, D.C.: National Education Association, 1952).

[4] John Dewey Society, *Democracy and the Curriculum* (New York: Appleton-Century-Crofts, Inc., 1939).

In *A Challenge to Secondary Education*[5] the Society indicated the nature of the critical and constructive thinking affecting secondary education. In *The Community School*[6] the relationship of the school —and especially its curriculum—to society was dealt with constructively. The Society for Curriculum Study was short-lived since it merged with the affiliate of the National Education Association peculiarly concerned with instructional leadership, the Supervisors and Directors of Instruction, in order to form a new, stronger organization called the Association for Supervision and Curriculum Development. This resulted in the formation of an organization dealing with curriculum improvement and one which had as a core group of its membership specialized personnel concerned with curriculum development. The new organization although less daring than the Society for Curriculum Study had much more impact because of the nature of its membership.

Research and experimentation in education. Institutions of higher education, state departments of education, voluntary educational associations (all supported in some instances by educational foundations) carried on research and educational demonstrations. Many of these projects dealt with youth and the secondary school.

Educational research as a concept was broadened. As it developed educational research changed in its nature and addressed itself to different types of problems. Even before the advent of "action research" the definition of educational research was stretched considerably. Barr's broad definition seems to cover adequately some of the imaginative projects carried out with the help of grants from private educational foundations during the depression and post-depression years. He defines educational research as:

> . . . any systematic striving for understanding actuated by a need or sensed difficulty directed toward some complex phenomenon of more than immediate personal concern stated in problematic form.[7]

Needless to say, broad field studies of the type that originated embodied curriculum development and greatly encouraged workers in this field to (a) increase their efforts and (b) make more use of research in problem solving.

The Eight-Year Study. The resistance of the secondary school to

---

[5] Samuel Everett, ed., *The Challenge to Secondary Education* (New York: Appleton-Century-Crofts, Inc., 1936).

[6] Samuel Everett, ed., *The Community School* (New York: Appleton-Century-Crofts, Inc., 1938).

[7] Chester W. Harris, ed., *Encyclopedia of Educational Research*, 3rd ed. (New York: The Macmillan Co., 1960), p. 1160.

change and the inhibitory influence of college admission requirements were emphasized by the new social situation. Both conditions
were challenged by a most significant study sponsored by the Progressive Education Association. Thirty senior high schools assisted
by a central staff and a number of other educational institutions
joined in what came to be called the Eight-Year Study. This study,
because of its scope, quality and timeliness, created a great deal of
ferment. It initiated a number of methods of curriculum study such
as the curriculum workshop, teacher-pupil planning and planned
evaluation of the curriculum development process and the effects of
new teaching-learning procedures on learners. It focussed attention
on curriculum change and careful evaluation in an unprecedented
manner. Its influence on educators, on teacher education, on educational thought, on the development of the evaluation movement, and
on further experimentation outweighed the fact that the direct objectives of the study were only partially achieved.

The Michigan Study of the Secondary School Curriculum, a
twelve-year study, and many individual school studies were direct
outgrowths of the Eight-Year Study.[8]

Increased use of research and demonstration. The practice of
using research money to finance massive, long-range attacks on educational problems spread widely. The projects carried out under
these grants were actually field studies which usually combined surveys of status, experimentation with new and untried educational
techniques, administrative adjustments and evaluation in one program. The total process was often called "demonstration research"
for the lack of a better name. Because of the tremendous involvement of people and institutions these studies were much more influential and impressive than the mere publication of recommendations.

The American Council on Education sponsored a nation-wide
study of teacher education. Several state studies of teacher education
were carried out. Studies of community school development, of
health education and of many special fields were made.

Faculty psychology, replication of traditional practices and reliance on administrative fiat receded well into the background.
Group thinking, group planning, research and the application of
research findings came to the fore. The importance of these developments are discussed elsewhere in the volume.

Educational expansion.   Education expanded into new areas

---

[8] Wilford M. Aikin, *The Story of the Eight-Year Study* (New York: Harper
& Row, Publishers, 1942).

largely through the influence of the federal government. The Civilian Conservation Corps was created to provide education, work and subsistence to older youth who were out of school and unemployed.

A more extensive movement was the adult education program administered by the Works Progress Administration. Operating under the sponsorship of established state and local education agencies the program had a wide import, especially on the development of adult education.

The emphasis on the needs of youth led to many youth activities sponsored by local schools often with the help of the National Youth Administration. Opportunity schools for youth and adults and even junior colleges sprang up. Youth service to the community was a fairly common development. Youth camps were established by various agencies. Camping as a part of the school program which had already been started in a few schools was given foundation support and carried out through the demonstration research process.

The emphasis on democratic processes.   John Dewey's stress on the importance of democratic education in a democratic society[9] finally began to be heeded. S. A. Courtis insisted on the general application of democratic principles to administration, to group effort in general and to the classroom. The experimentation that had been going on in a few centers was taken seriously. While most educational administrators and laymen had been skeptical previously, the change of social climate encouraged the spread of democratic school administration in schools. Democratic practices grew in the classroom; parents, teachers and learners increasingly participated in school administration and cooperative curriculum programs. Many teachers insisted on the right to participate in making all kinds of educational decisions from budget making to programming. The belief grew that basic, intelligent and widespread changes in behavior could be obtained best through the democratic administration of curriculum programs.

The spread of curriculum programs.   The earliest curriculum development programs were centered largely in public school systems. Since public education was legally a state function severe and just criticism was leveled at state departments of education for leadership failures. The combined result of the actual need and the persistent criticism was the rise and spread of state curriculum programs. The idea of involvement of many agencies in curriculum

---

[9] John Dewey, *Democracy and Education* (New York: The Macmillan Co., 1916).

development spread rapidly and was most effective at the state level. Most state curriculum programs became cooperative programs involving other state departments of government, teacher educating institutions, local school systems and unofficial or voluntary agencies. Educational foundations often aided these state programs with fiscal support. Michigan, as an example, received the aid of four different foundations during this period and carried out demonstration studies in many fields, all as aspects of a state curriculum program.

While state programs were important, the most significant development was the spread of curriculum development programs and actual program extension in local school systems both public and private. Typical developments in public school systems are reported in *Curriculum Improvement in Public School Systems.*[10]

The principal result of depression years on curriculum development was to bring about general acceptance of the need for curriculum change and the establishment of curriculum programs in most leading school systems both state and local. Private educational institutions and institutions of higher education were also affected and some excellent curriculum studies were carried out in these institutions. Colleges and universities, too, were gradually becoming the servants of the public; and while retaining the cultural subjects, they were constantly adding new ones to meet the increasing demands of modern complex conditions. The principle of continuous curriculum study was thus generally accepted by theorists and gradually put into practice in the field.

Clarifications of roles of curriculum workers. As curriculum development spread there was some confusion of roles. Those concerned with supervision were usually involved in curriculum revision and improvement from the first. There was, however, some confusion and apprehension when conservative supervisors and administrators realized that curriculum development implied fundamental criticism of both content and method followed by radical changes in method and curriculum. The possibilities of reorganizing educational systems and employing new types of specialists were also unsettling.

Supervision as a function of administration developed early. The function was stressed by Cubberley, Strayer, Engelhart, Briggs,

[10] Hollis L. Caswell and Associates, *Curriculum Improvement in Public School Systems* (New York: Bureau of Publications, Teachers College, Columbia University, 1950).

Hosic, Hillegas, Hanus and a number of other early educational leaders. Actually, Horace Mann laid the basis for supervision when he pointed out the weaknesses of the early American schools which were administered, and to a large extent taught, by laymen.

When large school systems emerged chief administrative officers were appointed to assist lay boards of control. At first, supervision was thought of as a role to be performed largely by school principals. The growth of large systems brought about the need for staff assistants to strengthen the central staffs. Supervisory positions increased more at the elementary school level than at the secondary level because of the factor of size, the nature of the curriculum at the different levels and the type of teacher preparation. A secondary teacher teaching a subject in which he was adjudged to be proficient did not seem to need much supervision and tended to resent it.

Nevertheless, supervision of an inspectorial type expanded steadily until about 1925. McKean and Mills provide us with background about this type of supervision:

> Thus the pattern of supervision as inspection to ascertain the deficiencies of teachers was established, and the early supervisor's role was based upon the premise that there were known and fixed methods of teaching which could be identified and judged by a brief observation of the teacher's work. If any consideration were given to the improvement of the teacher's work, it was based upon the assumption that an inspection might prompt the teacher to do better work. This early concept of supervision appears very narrow and inadequate in the light of our present knowledge of human growth and development. . . .[11]

During the decade of 1920–1930 the purpose and nature of supervision was brought into question. Hillegas and Hosic questioned the traditional assumptions the negative effects of supervision pointed out. Attempts were made to objectify the process of teaching and to appeal to the findings of educational research in order to ameliorate the authoritative aspects of supervision.

Curriculum development, to the extent that it existed, as well as curriculum policy enforcement and staff growth had been delegated pretty largely to directors of instruction and supervisors. These people had taken much of the load off the chief administrative officers and the school principals especially at the elementary school level. Their efforts were aimed primarily at coordination of school

---

[11] Robert C. McKean and H. H. Mills, *The Supervisor* (New York: The Center for Applied Research in Education, Inc., 1964), pp. 2–3.

practices in terms of administrative policy. While research findings were stressed to some extent and many good practices in staff growth were developing, the emphasis was still on teacher conformity to curriculum plans and teaching practices that were based largely on tradition and administrative fiat.

These practices were questioned and reoriented. Teachers were given leadership responsibilities, teachers helped set policies, and even the ideas and wishes of learners were given consideration. The new cooperative process became the norm in curriculum development even though many undesirable practices still remained in force. It became quite clear for the first time that effective curriculum change could best be obtained by a democratic process in which cooperation, creativity, respect for the individual and social responsibility are stressed.

The advent of creative and cooperative curriculum development changed the role of the supervisor. Almost everyone was involved in curriculum work in some role. The general supervisor gradually shifted into the role of a curriculum specialist. New curriculum specialists appeared. Many special supervisors disappeared but their places were taken by a host of special curriculum consultants. While the title of supervisor remained and while many exercised authority directly, roles and functions were changed. Even in systems using the supervisory concept supervisors were expected to help teachers identify problems, to help people to grow professionally and to help implement a democratic process of curriculum development. The emphasis on changing teacher behavior and on creative curriculum change increased and the stress on curriculum revision and curriculum construction declined.

The change of the role of the teacher from an operative who would put a new curriculum plan into effect to a responsible partner in a curriculum development program was fundamental. But other types of agents were brought in, such as the research technician who helped explain research findings and apply them to curriculum planning and teaching; the parent who helped plan; the non-parent who served as a resource person; and the administrator who administered the curriculum program. These changes along with the change in role of the supervisor to a consultant and curriculum leader were beneficial to everyone from the learner and teacher on the one hand to highest ranking administrator on the other.

Developments That Helped Set the Pattern

The big developments that helped fill out the modern concept of curriculum development may be summarized as follows:

1. Development of a closer relationship of the school to society and the individual learner;
2. Growth of the democratic processes, particularly participation of all of the partners in the enterprise and the development and wide use of new group processes;
3. The development of strong local programs of instructional improvement including curriculum development and in-service education of teachers as integrally or at least closely related programs;
4. The development of state curriculum programs; and
5. The increased interest and activity of the national government in education.

These developments will be discussed more fully in other chapters. Emphasis is being placed at this point on the growth of an idea and the methods needed to implement it, since the social, industrial and technical progress of the country imposed new obligations on educators. The most concise and authoritative statement of change in curriculum development is found in an official release[12] of the Association for Supervision and Curriculum Development. This statement stresses: (a) the change from faculty psychology to newer psychological theories, (b) the change from reliance on tradition and subjective judgment to a greater reliance on research, (c) changes in methods and materials, and (d) changes in patterns of participation in curriculum development. This concise and authoritative statement provides invaluable insight.

The precise nature of curriculum development is explained in the following chapter.

---

[12] Association for Supervision and Curriculum Development, *One Hundred Years of Curriculum Improvement,* 1857–1957 (Washington, D.C.: the Association, 1957).

CHAPTER III

Space Age Developments

In October 1957 the Union of Soviet Socialist Republics placed in orbit the first man-made satellite called "Sputnik." This event occurred in a world which was suffering from the aftermath of two devastating world wars—in a world which was engaged in a "Cold War" which had assumed the proportions of a life and death struggle. The flashing of the Sputnik across the skies brought about for the first time a clear perception of the meaning of recent, extraordinary scientific discoveries. Suddenly to many people came the meaning of Gerald Wendt's dictum that "the business of science is to make the present obsolete."[1] Suddenly people realized what scientists and technicians had been doing.

The shock of the striking change shook the educational world. Curriculum, teaching method, educational efficiency and curriculum development became front-page news for the first time. The schools were already undergoing great changes. Millions of postwar babies plus an increasing affluence had brought about the need for more and better school buildings, instructional materials and teachers. School authorities motivated by a belief in democracy and by the need for going to the people for higher taxes had involved an unprecedented proportion of the population in educational planning. However it was only a small proportion of citizens who knew what the pressing educational needs were and consequently felt a sense of personal participation in the educational venture.

Demands on Education

In addition to the problem of plant expansion two perennial problems of secondary education took on new dimensions. First, the public demanded a better quality of preparation for college-bound youth. Small high schools, poorly prepared teachers and obsolete subject matter were severely criticised. Second, the demand for a more extensive curriculum for non-college-bound youth strength-

---

[1] Gerald Wendt, Unpublished Manuscript.

ened. Better general education as well as better vocational offerings, particularly at the higher and more technical levels, were demanded. The need to hold more youth in secondary education was fully recognized. This need brought about a reconsideration of guidance programs and of vocational education for youth who would previously have left the high schools.

The demand for better science education. A third demand grew directly out of the sudden realization of the extraordinary power of science in bringing about change. This was a general demand for more and better science education. While the main stress was on science for college-bound youth the demand included a greater emphasis on science in general education at all levels and better science education for the non-college-bound youth in secondary schools.

What created the real confusion and enhanced the public debate on curriculum were the demands of those who felt that the schools should concentrate on producing an educational elite and the demands of those persons who criticised the schools for ulterior purposes, namely, to weaken public schools, as such, and to "keep taxes down." These two lines of attack were peculiarily effective in causing confusion because the egalitarian principle of curriculum planning in which each learner was to be administered to according to his needs seemed to be acceptable to educator and layman alike.

Critcisms of public education. Like the egalitarian principle the principle of public education supplemented by private effort seemed to be generally acceptable to most people in all of the states of the Union. The development of the Northwest Territory which saw the establishment of free, public secondary and higher education had set a pattern for developing areas and the basic principles of public education had been accepted in the older states.

Both the egalitarian curriculum principle and the public education principle were challenged overtly and covertly. There were many arguments for different and even opposing points of view. While some were against an extreme retrenchment in educational programs, others demanded innovations and reform. The task of deciding what an improved curriculum should be posed tremendous problems and precipitated endless debates. Yet the one thing about which all the people involved in this discussion were in agreement was that "yesterday's" education definitely no longer sufficed for "today." In the face of the many, and often conflicting, demands schools were called upon to justify their curriculums and their teaching effectiveness and also to make the educational reforms so urgently required by current social developments. Curriculum technicians and administrators were convinced that educational reforms were in order but did not wish to weaken progressive trends, i.e., "to throw the baby out with the bath," nor did they want to desert the principle of public education. The difficulty was increased by the development of strong, reactionary groups and movements designed to force a regressive direction on education. Hand and Sanford[2] stated the case very clearly for the "educationists" as leaders concerned with public school administration and general curriculum problems came to be called.

Criticism of education as a post-war phenomenon. Actually, the wave of criticism had originated prior to the appearance of Sputnik. It was basically a post-war phenomenon associated with the rapid technical and social changes of the period.

Position of non-public schools. Non-public schools were also placed in the position of reconsidering programs, methods and resources. Their problem was less severe, however, since their publics were of an "in-group" nature and also because the argument against higher taxes did not affect them unless they chose to use it for their own non-educational purposes.

The Public Debate on Curriculum

Curriculum became a matter of popular concern and curriculum development profited and grew as a result. Major and minor issues of curriculum development were discussed on the *front* pages of newspapers and in public forums of all kinds. The teaching of reading became a subject of discussion in public forums and in family circles. University graduates and virtual illiterates became experts on such issues as the "phonics method" of teaching reading and the desirability of making the American secondary school a selective institution.

Two groups of issues were raised, namely, educational issues in the field of public policy and technical issues in the field of research and curriculum development. In deciding on public policy society could only be helped by a widespread public debate on such an issue as the status and role of the education profession or the selectivity of the secondary school.

---

[2] Harold C. Hand and Charles W. Sanford, *The Bulletin,* XXXVII, No. 194 (Washington, D.C.: National Association of Secondary School Principals, 1953).

Actually the education profession had gone a long way in encouraging debate on public policy and had done much to involve parents and other citizens in public policy issues such as the purposes of education at the elementary and secondary level and the implications in terms of construction types, space requirements and unit costs for school buildings.

Debate on technical issues such as the "phonics method" of teaching reading or the use of television in direct teaching or the adding of a foreign language to the elementary school curriculum confronted school board members and educators with quite another problem. Difficulties of communication, the pressures of special interest groups, the time factor, the cost factor, and the lack of adequate research findings bearing on the problem under consideration made the situation difficult for all concerned. Responsible educational leaders realized that debate in some cases would benefit only the reactionaries and cause an insufferable attrition to the well of public confidence that existed. They had to face the augmentation of resources for expansion, for higher operating costs and for improving instruction in science or whatever the desirable reform might be.

The nature of the public policy issues. Five big issues in the field of public policy stood out.

The status of the education profession. Considerable progress had been made especially in the years 1946–1957 in improving the status of the profession.[3] Most administrators were possessors of degrees in administration. The preparation and licensure of teachers had been put on a professional basis and most states had made great progress in preparing and hiring teachers with minimal acceptable preparation in spite of the teacher shortage. Full-time curriculum specialists had considerable technical preparation although specialized advanced curriculums for curriculum specialists were just beginning to produce in any significant numbers.

After World War II salaries of teachers and other categories of educators were raised substantially. Deferred payments in the form of pensions were greatly improved. Fringe benefits were extended.

Many of these so-called improvements were questioned, particularly the increase in the proportion of professional courses and the strong role of the professional in curriculum development.

The seriousness of the issue was intensified by the battles from within. Critics of the education profession and its policies such as

---

[3] T. M. Stinnet, *The Profession of Teaching* (New York: The Center for Applied Research in Education, Inc., 1962).

those aligned with the Council for Basic Education indicated a genuine schism. More important to the situation was the bitter battle being waged between the teachers unions and the professional associations. These schisms were reflected in a weaker form among laymen too.

The purposes of education. While a fairly good consensus on the purposes of education had already been achieved in the United States, the public debate refined and extended the meanings of the general purposes. The necessity of meeting the needs of both the privileged and underprivileged became more apparent. The difficulty of adhering to idealistic democratic values and also catering to the gifted or privileged learner was better recognized by the layman. The importance of education as a cultural lever was highlighted.

The universalization of educational opportunity. The deterioration of living conditions in the hearts of the great cities, the conflict over civil rights, the community school development and, on the international scene, the foreign aid program for underdeveloped nations all tended to emphasize the need to universalize educational opportunity in terms of the needs and abilities of learners. Neither a bad educational beginning, nor race, nor accident of geographic residence, nor family income, nor special disabilities were considered to be justifications for educational deprivation. Only the stark absence of economic resources at a given time and place was considered as an adequate excuse for educational deprivation.

Probably the rapid expansion of junior or community colleges was the clearest evidence of the public policy drift toward universalization of opportunity in the United States. This very democratic and practical development occurred in spite of a very strong emphasis on the intellectualization of education which in turn led to the emphasis on the development of an educational elite.

The status of free public education. While the importance of education was clearly recognized during the great debate the status of free, public education remained unclear. Higher education probably lost ground except for junior college education which was largely public. The increase in the quality of junior college education, however, received little emphasis in spite of the expansion.

The tendency of elementary education to extend downward was temporarily stayed with the exception of the Head Start Program which was an experiment designed to remedy the cultural deprivations of children of low-income families. The kindergarten movement gained in some degree but usually lost out in competition for new funds.[4]

The hidden costs of secondary and higher education increased. Education seemed to be less, rather than more, related to society because of the great emphasis on subject matter mastery in context or out of context vis-a-vis community life.

The big question of using public funds for the exclusive support of public education stood out in bold relief.

As will be indicated later in the chapter, Congress moved to resolve the issue to some extent by passing very significant legislation in the period 1958–1965.

The role of local, state and national authorities. The perennial issue of local-state-federal relationships assumed a new urgency. Some states stressed educational leadership and educational support but gave great latitude to local districts in setting up the extent and the nature of the local instructional program. The wisdom of this policy was questioned by many spokesmen. Even the usefulness of local boards of education was questioned by some people. Many people demanded that the state guarantee an adequate program by establishing and enforcing educational standards in a very direct, authoritative manner.

Probably the major facet of the issue dealt with the role of the federal government in school support and in encouraging a more diversified school program through subsidies. Massive federal aid was called for by influential organizations while federal administrators and Congressmen tended to seek out specific projects for subsidization. Progress was often balked by disagreements about the extent and the nature of federal control which would accompany the proposed new programs.

In a report of the American Association of School Administrators Lindman discusses the role of the federal government as follows:

> Traditionally, the federal government's role in the partnership for public education has been basically noncoercive and supplementary. Except for the enforcement of federal policies pertaining to issues like civil rights and religious freedom, based upon the U.S. Constitution, federal action is limited to advice and financial contributions —both of which may be rejected by state and local school authorities.

---

[4] Neith Headley, *The Kindergarten: Its Place in the Program of Education* (New York: The Center for Applied Research in Education, Inc., 1965), pp. 22–27.

Within this framework the federal government, as a partner for public education, has contributed in many different ways. The federal government brings to the educational partnership a national point of view, the ability to focus attention of the nation upon the problems of education, a more efficient way to finance research and development work of common value to all states, a revenue potential unhampered by overdependence upon property taxation or by interstate economic competition. Finally, and most important, only the federal government can compensate for deficiencies in the school tax potential of low-income states and provide resources needed to improve school standards in these states.

But there are inherent limitations to the effectiveness of federal action in the field of education. Of the three partners, the federal government is farthest removed from the classroom where teaching and learning occur. Moreover, for the local board of education, education is the only problem; for state government, education is the major problem; for the federal government, education is one of many problems. Perhaps for this reason federal action in the field of education has, in many instances, been incidental to other federal concerns—national defense, full employment, or elimination of poverty.

Finally, federal categorical aids for special programs fail to recognize differences in educational needs in different communities. They are based upon the assumption that the most critical educational need is the same in all states.

Clearly the federal government can contribute much to public education. Some improvements in American education can be achieved only by federal action, and some can be greatly advanced by federal cooperation. But many important qualities of the public schools require vigorous state and local leadership that must be preserved in the emerging partnership.[5]

Nature of the technical issues. Four big technical issues in education were widely debated.

The problem of scope and balance. The sudden emphasis on certain subjects such as science and foreign language created a number of imbalances. For example, the peculiar choices of the student became less important and required courses regained much of their status. General education lost considerable impetus. The program of the student tended to become over-loaded with course work often only distantly related to his purposes. Certain emphases such as health, personal development and citizenship were vastly weakened.

---

[5] American Association of School Administrators, *The Federal Government and Public Schools* (Washington, D.C.: The Association, 1965), pp. 60–61.

These imbalances led to confusion and an emphasis on one part of a school program at the expense of other segments. Probably a more serious result was the element of insincerity that often intruded into the curriculum program. Administrators could scarcely be blamed for trying to make a "good showing" in science, physical fitness, or reading in the face of criticism by special interest groups.

The Association for Supervision and Curriculum Development produced a volume[6] which dealt with the problems of achieving and maintaining balance in the curriculum. Curriculum development is obviously concerned with the solution of these problems which must be recognized as ever-present in a changing society.

The space age developments of a technical and social nature indicated clearly the need for more intensive education in science, mathematics and the foreign languages. They indicated also, on second thought, the need for better social education and more emphasis on the arts and humanities. To some they indicated a need for a basic program of general education to replace "industrial arts education."

Many people saw the need only in terms of content. Therefore many projects were started with the purpose of deciding "what should be taught and when it should be taught." This was a recapitulation of early curriculum revision approaches. The problem of scope and balance was made more acute as were problems of administration, guidance and method.

The solution to some of the problems of scope and balance are reflected in later discussions of newer curriculum practices.

The nature of teacher education. Teacher education was roundly criticised for its failure to deal with the "explosion of knowledge," for its failure to provide students with adequate specialization, and for its failure to prepare students to use new methods. Part of the criticism came from subject-matter enthusiasts who felt they deserved special status or more time for specializing students. The issues were not new nor were the arguments one-sided. In many cases new and better accommodations were made. In many institutions interdepartmental cooperation was greatly improved.

Educators were, however, particularly challenged by a frontal attack on certification and professionalization as such. Instead of calling for better professional education, many critics took the position that professional education for a teacher was unnecessary or

---

[6] Association for Supervision and Curriculum Development, National Education Association, *Balance in the Curriculum*, 1961 Yearbook (Washington, D.C.: The Association, 1961).

even undesirable. This criticism had only a deleterious effect on teacher education since even those educators who were extremely critical of teacher education found the criticism rather irrational and destructive.

A foundation-supported report prepared by Dr. James B. Conant sought to define issues and make recommendations. This report, *The Education of American Teachers,*[7] certainly helped define issues but made many recommendations that were at odds with the practices in the field. The American Association of Colleges for Teacher Education, the National Educational Association and the National Council for the Accreditation of Teacher Education proceeded with their efforts to build a profession of teaching stimulated by and also hindered by the various countervailing influences.

Curriculum development was effected by the ferment in teacher education in many ways. Better preparation in both subject matter and professionalizing courses made for better teaching and better curriculum plans. The main negative effect was the emphasis on regression to earlier attitudes and practices. One principal remarked during a panel discussion of science teaching that she was glad she had never made any of the changes previously recommended in science education since the pendulum was swinging back. The impact of earlier changes such as changing from zoology and botany to a more integrated program called biology had already left her memory.

Stinnett[8] summarizes the problem of building a profession of teaching and spins out the various implications for education and for curriculum development.

The role of the layman in curriculum development. The role of the layman in curriculum development was not particularly controversial. But when such issues as methods of teaching reading, instruction by television, and methods of teaching science came up for public debate confusion reigned. School board members were asked to make decisions in the presence of powerful forces. The specialists were often not even consulted. The cooperative principle of operation was often violated. Usually a power struggle superseded debate and decisions were based on the outcome of the struggle.

Laymen, except those who were specialists in their own fields,

---

[7] James B. Conant, *The Education of American Teachers* (New York: McGraw-Hill Book Co., 1963).

[8] T. M. Stinnett, *The Profession of Teaching* (New York: The Center for Applied Research in Education, Inc., 1962).

such as scientists and engineers, were not involved in the new national curriculum projects until the effects of the project reached the local level.

School board members found themselves helplessly caught in the middle. They reacted strongly against professional pressures from the outside and from their own professional staffs. The National Association of School Boards made a strong effort for retaining the power of decision.

In the meantime forces at the national level were shaping up which would change the nature of the issue. Laymen in the national legislature found themselves deeply involved in making educational decisions.

The individualization of teaching. Individualization of teaching and curriculum planning was an accepted educational goal before the inception of the great debate. Suddenly educators found this goal challenged. Uniformity in content, fixed sequences, standardized methods and even a national curriculum were held up as desirable goals of curriculum development. The debate yielded few desirable results in this technical field of individualization.

The emphasis on research and understanding of human growth and development had had a profound influence on education and particularly on curriculum development. The curriculum at the nursery school, elementary school and junior high levels had come to use content as an instrument of individual development to a considerable extent. The nature of the learner, especially his growth pattern, was taken into account. Teacher-pupil planning and teacher-pupil-parent planning procedures developed. These procedures became a part of cooperative curriculum planning and produced a climate favorable to individualization. Grouping and categorizing learners lost favor when cooperative curriculum development based on the learner and his nature was practiced.

Many cities and some states had come out with developmental policies and curriculum plans in which procedures, goals and content were blended into a total scheme. The core curriculum procedure was a good example of the trend.

Needless to say these newer procedures came under close and unsympathetic scrutiny and research and experimentation became even more difficult.

Results of the Public Debate

A decade of public debate had considerable influence on American education and on curriculum development. Certainly public interest was heightened. Citizen responsibility increased. The immensity of the educational problem in the United States was indicated by the remarkable growth in organizations interested in *all* aspects of education. Curriculum issues became more meaningful. Public policy issues such as source and amount of funds for education stood out. Public media devoted much time and space to education. Participation in voting tax support for the purpose of increasing the quantity and quality of education enlightened citizens in many ways. Unfortunately the debate was often acrimonious, unethical and destructive. School administrators and curriculum specialists often did their work in an atmosphere which was unfriendly to honest effort, careful deliberation and experimentation.

Nevertheless, education moved forward. In response to the criticism schools engaged in almost a complete reorientation of science curriculums. Education became more selective but at the same time new programs for secondary school students who would otherwise leave school were pushed vigorously. New programs were provided for the mentally retarded and other learners with exceptional needs. The community school movement continued to make headway.

In regard to the issue of curriculum balance, most educators and laymen became convinced that all educational objectives must be served. Studies of the learning process, of classroom organization, of curricular areas such as mathematics were vigorously pursued. New developments in subject-matter areas received much lay support.

Changes in the curriculum and curriculum development. While curriculum balance seemed to lose out in the period of conflict and change there were many significant and desirable developments in materials of instruction, in reorganization and updating of content in subject areas, in teaching method and in research. Through fellowships for selected, experienced teachers the leadership personnel was augmented and the quality of teaching was strengthened. These curriculum changes are discussed in a later chapter.

Thus education moved forward in a turbulent situation. Curriculum specialists found their roles confused but actually enhanced. More, rather than less, specialists were employed to do research, to plan curriculums, to plan lessons, to prepare materials, to help teachers in the classroom, to teach television classes and to advise lay boards of control and administrators in regard to the many technical problems of teaching and curriculum.

Many special developments appeared but the *basic underlying trends* in teaching and curriculum development continued. Many of the public policy and technical issues remained to be decided in the ensuing years.

The participation of the federal government.   The federal government moved swiftly to resolve some of the public policy issues by appropriating vast sums of money under the anti-poverty program, under the National Defense Education Act, under various acts designed to promote vocational education, under acts which made money available for educational research, and under the monumental Elementary and Secondary Education Act of 1965.

Broad educational planning in the form of surveys, curriculum development and in-service education increased when the federal government made itself a major partner in the educational venture. In spite of the mandatory nature of some of the new legislation there was much curriculum development called for in developing sequential programs in such fields as science, foreign language and the social studies—in planning new programs for the under-privileged —in fitting vocational education to the labor market—in using new techniques such as team teaching and television teaching.

Lastly, as can well be imagined, the roles of the local-state-federal educational agencies were significantly changed by the federal involvement which first reached a significant proportion at the end of 1965.

CHAPTER IV

Basic Concepts of Curriculum Development

Curriculum development is the focal aspect of the research and development function in any educational system. As such curriculum development is inextricably intertwined with research, with the planning of new programs, with educational experimentation, and with staff growth activities. Effective curriculum development depends to a very great extent on the factors involved in staff morale such as growth in teaching performance, staff solidarity, staff continuity, selection and induction procedures, and on staff participation in the administration of the total educational endeavor.

Curriculum development depends so much on in-service education which is so closely related to curriculum development that it may aptly be called the Siamese twin of curriculum development. Practically all of the curriculum development activities of a program form a part of the in-service education program of a school or school system. Curriculum development cannot expand without good in-service education. Curiously enough, in-service education is not similarly dependent on curriculum development. Many school systems have fairly effective in-service education programs which never face up to developing new teaching-learning procedures and putting them to work in a systematic manner.

Concepts of Curriculum Development

While the practices of curriculum development show considerable variation, certain basic concepts underly the practices. Principal among these are a certain concept of change, a concept of strategy or of democratic educational leadership and a well-defined concept of process.

The concept of change. Change is accepted as necessary and desirable. Change in this context refers to change in man's knowledge of human learning, to change in values and social systems and to change in the actual program of the educational system. There are no good static programs of education—this has to be strongly emphasized. The high school principal who stated that he was glad he had not fallen for the idea of changing his very fundamentalist program is an anachronism just as is the school superintendent who tries to ride out his last five years on his old set of practices.

Curriculum development is designed to cope effectively with changes in the school's setting, to utilize wisely the new technology of education, to contribute some program research to that technology, and to express the growing wisdom of the human race by updating objectives and planning a balanced educational program for meeting them successfully.

The Nature of Curriculum Change

The sensitivity to the need for curriculum change increased sharply in the post-war period of 1945–1965. Each year there was significant growth. In 1965 a report[1] dealing with the phenomenon of curriculum change was published. It examined many problems, proposed typical models of curriculum development process, suggested needed research and defined issues. Many implications of the report could be pointed out but three seem to be especially pertinent: (1) the sensitivity to the need for curriculum change is high, (2) there is no agreement on strategy, and (3) the essential process of curriculum development is not widely understood, accepted and trusted to bring about needed change. Yet the analysis which is completely friendly to curriculum development as commonly defined did not indicate that curriculum development if fully and properly implemented in any school system could not care for all of the problems of change that were raised. Lippitt's pivotal issue is *apropos:*

> . . . I think that there will develop, even more sharply than there is now, a period of conflict over the problems, the possibilities, the dangers of the teacher-free curriculum concept, the concept of the teaching-learning process carried by materials with minimal interference by teachers. There is a tremendous challenge, certainly, in the explosion of communication technology; yet I predict that there will be developed a far more significant, more professional role for the teacher because of this fact rather than a diminishing role. The teacher should become a key diagnostic agent on individual needs for learning, should become a planner and designer of individualized learning activities, should become a trainer and a supervisor of the human resources used in the classroom.[2]

---

[1] Association for Supervision and Curriculum Development, *Strategy for Curriculum Change* (Washington, D.C.: The Association, 1965).

[2] *Ibid.*, pp. 27–28.

Naturally this concept of change has many implications for the role of curriculum workers, for administration and for the preparatory programs for teachers and educational specialists.

The concept of democratic leadership. The concept of strategy refers to democratic educational leadership so necessary to curriculum development. But this must not be confused with earlier concepts of the administrator or supervisor as the educational leader. The concept of broad, democratic educational leadership refers to the activities of citizens' committees, of classroom teacher organizations, of curriculum committees, of publishers of educational materials, of designers of educational facilities and of all who work for the attainment of educational goals they believe in.

Nowhere is this concept better stated than in the 1960 Yearbook of the Association for Supervision and Curriculum Development.[3] The authors defined educational leadership as *"that action or behavior among individuals or groups which causes both the individual and the groups to move toward educational goals that are increasingly mutually acceptable to them."*

The same authors in the same chapter define the tasks as follows:

Task I. To Help the People of the School Community Define Their Educational Goals and Objectives.

Task II. To Facilitate the Teaching-Learning Process—Develop Greater Effectiveness in Teaching.

Task III. To Build a Productive Organizational Unit.

Task IV. To Create a Climate for Growth and the Emergence of Leadership.

Task V. To Provide Adequate Resources for Effective Teaching.

The above statement comprises both a concept and a job analysis. This concept implies a programmatic approach as against a specious or unplanned approach. It also implies a value-based democratic approach rather than a mechanistic "front office" approach. This democratic approach means that curriculum development lies at the *base* of the educational effort to forge the bonds of common citizenship, to harness the energies of the people, and to develop the natural resources of the country. It implies a total staff involvement rather than "curriculum department" or supervisory initiative. It implies that instructional specialists fit into a program. *A priori*

---

[3] Association for Supervision and Curriculum Development, National Educational Association, *Leadership for Improving Instruction,* 1960 Yearbook, (Washington, D.C.: The Association, 1962), Chapter 2.

definition of roles of specialists is played down and teamwork based first on the program objectives and on the unique abilities of specialists is convincingly implied.

The concept of process. Consonant with the other two basic concepts is the concept of process. Basically, schools and curriculums change as society changes. Thus all curriculums are in a process of change to some extent even though the change seems at times imperceptible. Even the senior high school curriculum which in most countries is conservative finds itself enormously changed in recent years. This is one meaning that grows out of the concept of process.

Another meaning may be referred to as the creative concept of curriculum itself. Zirbes expresses it well in her italicized manner.

> *Creatively considered, a curriculum is an outgoing continuity of situational "school" experiences—in which teachers are interacting educatively with learners in terms of the needs, potentialities, and propensities of learners, on the one hand, and, on the other hand, in terms of the cultural conditions, resources, and interactive processes by which learners are actually challenged and zestfully involved. . . .*[4]

So curriculum development is a process for improving the processes of development, testing and using better teaching-learning procedures. American experience has demonstrated that these procedures can only be brought to a high level of effectiveness in the field, as opposed to the laboratory, through creative and democratic approaches, and the result was *the* educational explosion, the sound of a roaring pursuit of learning that has never been matched either in quality or in numbers in U.S. history.

Utilization of Group Processes

Administration has had many interpretations in human affairs. These range from traditional concepts of leadership in tightly structured primitive societies through various types of dictatorships, through various modern interpretations of a managerial nature to a rationalized democratic administration resting on an extensive use of group processes or group dynamics referred to in Chapter I. The democratic interpretation seems to be peculiarly adapted to the solution of the kinds of problems faced by educational leadership in

---

[4] Laura Zirbes, *Spurs to Creative Teaching* (New York: G. P. Putnam's Sons, 1950), pp. 90–91.

the changed society of the twentieth century. While considerable authoritarianism remained in educational administration a surprising spread of democratic practices occurred after 1930. The use of democratic principles was not confined to any one problem area in education but in the field of curriculum development democratic or cooperative operations were inherent. Group processes were essential to the successful achievement of defined educational purposes. This probably grew out of the nature of the profession of teaching and the fact that the public was so directly involved in education.

Classroom teaching and administrative processes were greatly enriched through the scientific study of group processes or group dynamics. This contribution of social psychology explained many things such as the importance of perception, the need for good human relations, the failure of authoritative approaches to curriculum development and, most significantly, the potential release of power through a wise and natural use of group processes. Once perceived and rationalized, group processes were widely used in curriculum planning. Trow's[5] analysis of group processes and especially his explanations of applications to the field of educational leadership indicate the essential role of group process.

Robert Bills begins with the basic assumption that ". . . change is a normal aspect of human growth and development and that a condition of 'no change' represents the atypical. . . ."[6] He then sets up certain conditions that should be provided to accelerate change. He proposes that anyone such as a volunteer leader or a status administrator should provide these conditions and be guided by their importance.

The conditions he prescribes may be paraphrased as follows:

1. The individual must desire to change.
2. Anyone providing leadership must accept without anxiety or falsehood the concern of the other person.
3. Anyone providing leadership must experience a positive and unconditional regard for the worth of the people with whom he works.
4. Anyone providing leadership must experience an empathic understanding of how the other person feels and what he is experiencing and he must attempt to communicate his positive and unconditional regard and empathic understanding for the other person to him and, lastly, the other person must receive this communication of positive and unconditional regard and empathic understanding.

---

[5] Chester W. Harris, ed., *Encyclopedia of Educational Research,* 3rd ed. (New York: The Macmillan Co., 1960), pp. 602–12.

[6] Robert Bills, *People and Progress* (Unpublished manuscript, College of Education, University of Alabama).

Few curriculum workers express themselves in such a sophisticated manner as does Bills but his statement expresses remarkably well what process-minded curriculum workers believe.

The way group process is used in groups studying education is described and rationalized in detail by Kelley[7] in his book on workshop method.

Most current reports of curriculum development show how group process is used in the field. Its rationale and use in a state curriculum program are explained in *Curriculum Improvement in Public School Systems.*[8]

Receiving impetus from the demonstration research studies, the idea of democratically conducted working groups meeting in situations where informal relationships exist has taken hold in connection with every activity of the program. Through the use of this technique thousands of teachers, research specialists, administrators, specialists from community and extra-community agencies, and laymen have become a part of the program. Hundreds of these conferences take place, involving from 25 to 150 people at a time. They last from two days to six weeks. More and more they are being sponsored by individuals and voluntary groups. A hundred or so, depending upon definition, are sponsored each year by institutions of higher education. Another hundred or so are sponsored by voluntary agencies, and when no voluntary agency has assumed the responsibility the central committees of the program usually provide the sponsorship or co-sponsorship and the dynamic leadership.

Pre-planning committees, fairly large in number, are usually appointed. The conference is generally announced solely in terms of a purpose rather than in terms of a program. Ofttimes outlines of the program or agenda are prepared shortly before the workshop convenes, but sometimes no agenda are prepared in advance at all, and the group sets up the program on the ground.

The problem census, the very brief discussion group designed to start participation, the continuing study or production group, the stimulatory panel discussion, the general session designed to appraise the conference and to plan next steps, the use of first names, the obvious presence of the peer relationship, recreational activities such as fishing and folk dancing, and the "bull session"—these are some of the earmarks of a Michigan workshop.

The central planning and appraisal groups in the program rate the workshop method as the most promising of all methods.

---

[7] Earl C. Kelley, *The Workshop Way of Learning* (New York: Harper & Row, Publishers, 1957).

[8] Hollis L. Caswell and Others, *Curriculum Improvement in Public School Systems* (New York: Bureau of Publications, Teachers College, Columbia University, 1950), pp. 407–409.

The Workshops Are Used as a Way of Initiating a Program

Many school administrators have very deliberately used the workshop to prepare the nucleus of leadership in the local faculty for attacking some particular curriculum problem. In this case a few teachers who will later be carrying out new programs such as core curricula and the like have been selected to attend certain workshops. Sometimes this number of teachers is increased from year to year so that a sizable block of faculty becomes prepared through workshop experience. Tentative plans for the local curriculum project are developed and the understandings and skills of personnel are increased at the workshop. The activity is than transplanted to the local school and runs its natural course of success or failure. Appraisal of this activity indicates that it greatly increases the chances of success of any given instructional procedure.

Workshops Are Constantly Appraised by Participants

Various efforts have been made to appraise the conference or workshops. The following quotation from the Annual Report of the Subcommittee on Better Human Relations indicates the kind of rough appraisal that is often attempted:

	No. of Persons Checking
Acceptable conference	5
Helpful conference	19
Very helpul conference	10
Inadequate conference	0

Members have reported these things which bothered them during a conference:

Not enough administrators present.
Need for better definition of goals.
Conference too well-structured beforehand.
Too much participation from few—little from many.
Too much conversion, not enough concept regarding ways to help people understand the problem of human relations.

Members reported these things as the most satisfying:
General friendliness.
Good relationships between groups and individuals.
Freedom and easy exchange of ideas.
Opening and closing sessions.
The indications of emerging leadership in the field of human relations.

Sometimes appraisal is conducted on a much more scientific basis. Extensive efforts have been made to follow up persons in their local situations months after the workshop has occurred. The upshot of all this appraisal is seen in the wide usage of the workshop method and in the strong beliefs that individuals have in its potency. Story after story comes to light of persons who have had their entire careers changed by a three-day experience in one of these workshops. The democratically conducted workshop has become something of an article of faith on the part of the group which is active in the program.

This great emphasis on process was reinforced by a new emphasis on an old phenomenon, namely, that of perception—its mechanics and its relation to personal behavior and growth.

The concept of perception. The applications of this development to education and curriculum development are adequately explained by Combs, Kelley and others in the 1962 Yearbook of the Association for Supervision and Curriculum Development.[9] Kelley attempted to derive the entire curriculum from a perceptual basis in his fascinating volume entitled *Education for What Is Real.*[10] The child development movement put an emphasis on reality as opposed to assumptions about the effectiveness of certain social and educational controls.

Other applications of the perceptual theory have been referred to in Bills' conditions for change in this chapter and in the author's definition of the curriculum as the learner's environment in action in Chapter I.

These three basic concepts—change, leadership and process— had their beginnings earlier but the decade of the 1960's saw their fruition research-wise and also their wide application in curriculum development.

Determinants of the Curriculum

Curriculum development takes place in a social context, hence it is always subject to political action—and rightly so. It would be meaningless to state that education should serve the community or be influenced by the needs and wishes of a specific culture unless political action were recognized. It would be—to say the least— contradictory to maintain that schools were instrumentalities for teaching citizenship and at the same time to maintain that the curriculum should be entirely remote from political forces and circumstances. Thus *two* major educational tasks have faced our educational authorities: to *extend* educational opportunity to the people

9 Association for Supervision and Curriculum Development, National Education Association, *Perceiving—Behaving—Becoming,* 1962 Yearbook (Washington, D.C.: The Association, 1962).

10 Earl C. Kelley, *Education for What Is Real* (New York: Harper & Row, Publishers, 1948).

and to *reshape* the curriculum to meet the *modern* needs of our society.

Mackenlzie[11] deals with the issue pragmatically when he states that curricular decisions are influenced by four forces, namely, (a) individuals and organizations, (b) legal agencies, (c) educationists and educators, and (d) students. These forces in action explain how education meets the needs and wishes of its society. When an authoritative state agency decrees that all pupils shall be taught how to drive a motor vehicle it is readily seen that society has expressed itself through a very complex process. Still, the principle stands— *curriculum development finds one of its sources in the nature of society,* which includes the values that the society cherishes and wants perpetuated. In the United States this clearly refers to the values that are characteristic of a free, open society. Often these values are more ideal than real but they represent goals nevertheless.

Likewise when a powerful social and educational movement arises designed to carry all youth through the secondary school even though the curriculum must be changed to meet their needs a second principle is at work in addition to the first. *Curriculum development finds one of its sources in the nature and needs of the learner.*

Naturally, different people see things differently. Some people feel education is too much concerned with meeting the simple but important life needs of pupils. As the dimensions of the expansion of knowledge became obvious and as the importance of the exact sciences to a space-oriented world was highlighted by spectacular space ventures many people became increasingly concerned about curricular issues. Some for good reasons and others for specious reasons insisted that the principal disciplines had been forgotten, that they were under-emphasized, but there was general *consensus* that the curriculum has to be constantly improved and better methods of instruction developed. There was also a general consensus that in view of the urgent need for *specialists* in a Space Age technology the system of higher education, especially in the field of science *had* to be reorganized as a result of strong public pressure.

And, indeed, they had considerable cause for concern. The causes were essentially these:

1. Population expansion was straining education as was the attempt

---

[11] Association for Supervision and Curriculum Development, National Education Association, *What Are the Sources of the Curriculum? A Symposium* (Washington, D.C.: The Association, 1962), pp. 72–80.

to expand universal education to the educationally under-privileged. Money, equipment and facilities were in short supply.

2. The contribution of the subject matters such as mathematics had
not been re-integrated into modern curriculums nor brought up to
date with recent developments in the discipline.

3. The teacher education curriculum was overloaded even though
teachers were required to spend ever-increasing numbers of years
in higher education.

4. Educators found it difficult to deal realistically with very unrealistic
criticisms and demands on the schools. Students, parents, teachers
and professors responded to different perceptions, needs and pressures so that confusion was rife.

5. Neither the cost nor the nature of quality education had been properly analyzed, understood and presented.

The Emphases on the Disciplines

The early 1950's gave birth to many criticisms of the schools
charging laxness in stressing the basic disciplines. The storm raged
around history, an old focus for curricular strife, around the sciences, around mathematics and also the foreign languages. This
debate resulted in two major developments affecting mainly elementary, secondary and teacher education.

On the side of the disciplines responsible leaders set up massive
studies which were essentially curriculum movements. The disciplines of science, mathematics and foreign language received substantial material support from industry, government and the educational foundations and, consequently from the efforts made by curriculum specialists.

Professional educators usually dubbed as "educationists" by their
critics, made determined efforts to communicate and cooperate with
the disciplinary groups. Teacher education groups, administrative
groups and especially the Association for Supervision and Curriculum Development sought to bring about a balanced emphasis on the
meeting of all of the educational needs of the society. A great deal
of attention was given in professional circles to the nature of organized knowledge and its implications for the curriculum.

The results of all of these efforts brought about desirable results.
They fell into four principal areas: (a) the development of useful
cooperation between subject-matter specialists, school administrators and curriculum specialists, (b) updating of subject matters, (c)
in-service education of subject-matter teachers in both content and
method, and (d) increased resources for teaching the subject mat-

ters including new teaching equipment such as television and the teaching machine, more instructional supplies, more consultants and more teachers.

One new development in the nature of a curriculum invention resulted. This was the tendency to use the organized subject matters in adapted forms for specialized education at the senior high school and junior college level for both those preparing to specialize through a college career and those preparing to enter into some vocation of a technical, sub-professional nature.

The effects of the attempts to organize curricula around the disciplines in elementary education were not so clear. The new procedures were mainly experimental in nature. Reading as a tool received more emphasis. New approaches to science and mathematics were developed. Only the experiments such as those in mathematics and foreign language could be thought of as disciplinary in nature.

Evaluating Curriculum Development

Evaluation of curriculum development deals principally with four problems. At times it becomes necessary to take an objective look at the status of a given curriculum. Usually qualitative and quantitative aspects are considered. Score cards are often used, such as Herrick's checklist on citizenship.[12]

In this technique the user of the checklist is asked whether all basic issues have been considered and expressed, one way or another, whether all methods have been considered and selections made therefrom, and whether all sorts of teaching aids have been considered. The book includes a general discussion of all aspects of education for citizenship and thus may serve as a guide to the use of the checklist.

Another common and useful form of evaluation is the problem census. Such evaluation seeks to locate "sore spots." The element of the feelings of teachers, of citizens, of students are commingled with objective data. Such evaluation is very useful in setting up work schedules, in appointing committees and in determining timing and emphasis.

The third common form of evaluation is the evaluation of characteristics and short-term outcomes. For instance, many institutions

---

[12] Theral T. Herrick, *School Patterns for Citizenship Training* (Ann Arbor: The University of Michigan, 1947).

re-program and re-assign tasks to individuals on an annual basis. Increasingly such re-programming is preceded by the gathering of objective data on student achievement, on parent opinions, on teacher reactions and various other data. These data are then collated and interpreted by administrators, by curriculum councils, by individual curriculum committees and by participants as a total group in some cases. An example of the latter is the "evaluation day" technique that is used by some school systems. In this technique the entire professional staff with such consultant help as it chooses goes into session for a day or two to assess progress and to determine the basis for continuing curriculum development.

An example of short-term evaluation. The ultimate objective of any good local curriculum program must, of course, always be better learning. This breaks down into the improvement in the scope and variety of learning opportunities on the one hand and the improvement of the quality of instruction on the other. Evaluation, however, cannot always be carried on through direct measurement of the ultimate objective. Consequently, it is necessary to set up a number of pragmatic criteria with which to examine any curriculum program such as the following:

1. Is your curriculum program comprehensive in that it deals with the entire program of the community school and at the same time "broken front" in that it isolates certain problems of high priority and moves to the solution of those problems?

2. Is your curriculum program realistic, i.e., does it stem from the real nature of society with its persistent life problems; from the real nature of the human organism and its ways of learning and growing?

3. Does your curriculum program tend to implement generally the democracy principle, i.e., does it seek to democratize the social life of the school, the teaching processes of the school, and the administration of the school?

4. Does your curriculum program seek to implement the package of findings referred to as child development findings by setting up new instructional organization, i.e., continuing primary unit where the teacher stays with the children for three years; or the development of basic and continuing case studies of learners to be passed on and used from level to level; or the development of the self-contained classroom, e.g., a room where one teacher has the total responsibility for the instruction of one group of children with the

help of such resources from a school system and community as may be available?

5. Is your curriculum program cooperative in nature, i.e., are the decisions as what to work on and how to work on it made by the cooperative machinery of the curriculum program or by some functionary?

6. Does your curriculum program seek to round out the scope of service of the community school, i.e., does it seek to extend the school program upward and downward to meet legitimate learning needs of children and citizens? Does it seek to broaden the offerings of the secondary program to increase the holding power of secondary education through the meeting of all of the needs of all of the children?

7. Does your curriculum program result in effective professional growth in teachers?

8. Does your curriculum program develop leadership in your system?

9. Does your curriculum program tend to clarify the real purpose of education?

10. Does your curriculum program bring about more realistic evaluation of teaching efforts and of curriculum?

11. Does your curriculum program result in new instructional policies, new resource units and new cooperative teaching plans?

Long-term evaluation is needed. Many of the best results of curriculum development efforts are not susceptible to evaluation on a short-term basis. Major projects require periods of up to ten years for redesigning, retooling, testing of new teaching-learning procedures, preparation of new resource materials and in some cases even the re-education of teachers. Consequently some evaluation activities deal with long-term outcomes.

Outcomes themselves grow out of objectives modified by the changes in emphases that creep into a complex operation. The nature of short-term and long-term outcomes is treated in *Curriculum Improvement in Public School Systems*.[13]

---

[13] Hollis L. Caswell, *et al., Curriculum Improvement in Public School Systems* (New York: Bureau of Publications, Teachers College, Columbia University, 1950), Chapter 5.

CHAPTER V

Organization and Services for Curriculum Development

Organization for curriculum development depends largely on the organization of education in any given political unit. In many countries the responsibility for education rests with the nation-state. In such states education is typically centralized and carried out by various kinds of municipalities which are strictly creatures of the state designed to carry out the wishes of the central government. For instance in the USSR although education is in the hands of the Commissariats for Education of the Constituent and Autonomous Republics—the higher educational and scientific institutions in the autonomous republics are *subordinate* to the Commissar for Education in Moscow who has an exclusive, undivided *control* over the development of curriculum, *exceedingly influenced* by the basically rigid but frequently changing *Communist Party* line. In federated countries, however, education is often a constitutional responsibility of the member states subject to constitutional limitations only. Such states, in turn, choose to keep the power or to delegate the power to intermediate or local school districts. In the United States the federated states are highly centralized as in Alaska, Hawaii and Delaware; decentralized into firmly controlled school districts as in New York or decentralized into semi-autonomous school districts as in the Midwestern states.

In the Federal Republic of Germany the authority of the states over education is supreme. After years of functioning with an extra-legal council there was set up by agreement an Educational Council constituted with official membership from the federal government and the various states. The functions of the council are to be: (1) drafting plans for developing the German educational system in correlation with developments in the cultural, economic and social spheres; (2) seeking ways to meet the increasing demand for highly qualified men and women in the society as a whole; (3) making proposals for structural changes in the educational system; (4) calculating the costs of such reforms.

In spite of the constitutional provision that places authority over education in the German state rather than the federal government curriculum development seldom takes place in spite of efforts to promote it because of the nature of the culture and the policies of the various state parliaments and ministries of education and culture.

Australia is an example of a federation which permits state systems of education. While curriculum development is permitted and occurs to some extent at the state level it fails to thrive because of unfavorable cultural attitudes.

India has a federal system operating, at present, under a one-party government. States have considerable authority and the federal government encourages education and curriculum development. It has created the National Council for Educational Research and Training concerned mainly with (a) developing educational policy, (b) preparing education leaders, and (c) encouraging curriculum development and experimentation. Still, in spite of latitude and encouragement, little curriculum development occurs at any level. Nevertheless, the National Council and the Educational Council created in Germany have real possibilities for curriculum development and the outcome will be watched by all countries.

The Soviet Union operates educational programs through its various republics and puts a great emphasis on education and curriculum change. The authoritarian government which carries out the policies of the one-party scheme mandates arbitrarily the educational reform through its various agents. Thus no real curriculum development occurs even though major and swift changes in curriculum are brought about.

International developments and developments in all countries will depend to a great extent on curriculum changes in the next few years, for proper education is nowadays the most important *single factor* in achieving not only rapid economic development and technological progress but *also* in creating a social order founded on the values of freedom, social justice, and equal opportunity. It is futile to suggest the role of curriculum development in the various cultural situations that exist. It is clear that curriculum development is now to be associated inextricably with educational and cultural situations where educational responsibility is diffused and where individual initiative and democratic administration prevail. On the other hand, curriculum development is incompatible with centralization of educational authority.

Since there are other factors at work such as leadership, policy, attitudes and resources the extent and nature of curriculum development does not vary *only* with the factor of administrative organization and control, but centralization of authority is a major factor.

The Favorable Climate for Curriculum Development

Approaching the matter empirically it can be said that curriculum development thrives in the semi-autonomous local district because in this situation it is an *essential* and a *creative* function. It deals with meeting the learning needs of individual learners in a given cultural situation. The factors are real. The interplay of forces is understandable. The same people who develop curriculum plans execute them. Change is perceived as a continuum because of the nature of the situation and the continuity of the leadership.

The fact that curriculum development in its full form and function is found in local school districts of a semi-autonomous nature does not mean that curriculum development should not and could not take a place in an intermediate district, in a federated state or in a centralized nation-state. The same need for changing curriculum and method exists in all schools.

Administrative Policy and Curriculum Development

All school districts are to some extent parts of a greater whole. Some powers are always reserved. Some conditions must always be met. Most of the legal conditions are set by the state department of education or its counterpart as a result of legislative mandate or administrative judgment. Therefore, the state department of education plays an important role in curriculum development. If the state department of education provides educational leadership with a minimum of education control its role is considerably enhanced. In general, the role of the local education authority in curriculum is enhanced, not hindered, by state leadership.

Curriculum development requires administrative direction and support at any level. Krug stresses the importance of administration to curriculum development:

> Curriculum planning requires those services and arrangements known as administration—the selection, assignment, stimulation, guidance, and evaluation of human effort.

Democratic curriculum planning particularly requires effective administrative services and arrangements, for it includes the participation of many individuals and groups in the study of issues and the making of decisions.[1]

The legislative role of the board of education.   The primary responsibility, then, of a chief administrative official is to help his board to develop and legislate a public policy dealing with curriculum development. This policy does not need to be complete or detailed; in fact, it is better if it is not too detailed. But it should state the values to be sought, the locus of responsibility for various functions and the basic organization for curriculum development. For instance, the policy should include such things as the qualitative level to be sought, a position on experimentation and evaluation, the roles of administrative officers, of curriculum workers and of the teachers.

A good example occurred when a certain local authority made a decision in designing buildings and curriculum for its new secondary schools. It instructed its chief administrative officer to design its buildings and curriculum around a generalized approach to the sciences rather than a departmentalized approach. No money or effort was to be spared in educating the students in the field of science. All other planning from the point of the policy decision forward was left to the staff.

Unfortunately, the *public* policy aspect of curriculum development received little emphasis through the years which accounted to some extent for the chaos in the post-Sputnik period.

It is of great importance that a board of education take an aggressive but friendly, helpful and legislative posture in regard to curriculum development. The activity is too important and too technical to be turned over to staff members and laymen without any ground rules for the achieving of proper, universal education is not solely a financial or administrative problem; it is *also* a matter of *overcoming* traditional social attitudes, cultural deprivation, and communal tensions arising especially in our country from differences of language, religion and ethnic origin. Therefore the activity is so important that professional shortsightedness or whim cannot be tolerated. Hence a wise board of education adopts a policy and sees that it is followed.

---

[1] Edward A. Krug, *et al., Administering Curriculum Planning* (New York: Harper & Row, Publishers, 1956), p. 1.

Organization of the Curriculum Development Program

Even in a small school district some special organization of personnel is necessary to make the curriculum development program definitive and effective. In larger and more complex units the need for organization is still more crucial.

Alice Miel sets forth the most desirable characteristics of organization:

> Although it must be admitted that organization cannot of itself guarantee security, growth, and accomplishment, the desirable type of organization can make a significant contribution to deliberate social change. The following appear to be the characteristics of a desirable organization:
>
> 1. It is functional.
> 2. It facilitates widespread participation and a free-flowing type of interpersonal relationships.
> 3. It fulfills a constructive social purpose that is the group's own purpose.
> 4. It provides for continuity of problem-solving.
> 5. It provides for necessary coordination among groups.[2]

Organization and the nature of curriculum development. Effective organization must be based on the nature of curriculum planning. As has been indicated, planning is influenced by many intrinsic and related factors. Saylor and Alexander make clear the nature of the activity by describing the principal levels of curriculum planning:

> Four levels of curriculum planning may be identified. Of first importance is the teachers' own planning—both with and without pupils—of the curriculum of his particular groups of learners. It is at this level that curriculum planning directly affects the experiences of learners. Regardless of how sound planning at other levels may be, it serves little purpose unless it is implemented at the classroom level. Curriculum planning at this level is basically a matter of making choices within a flexible curriculum framework. This is the level with which Part 4 of this book dealt.
>
> Second, there is the school unit level. The building faculty, perhaps together with pupils and parents, is responsible for planning the total program of the school for effecting desired learnings. Here planning may proceed through the total faculty, departmental and grade groups, special committees, and cooperative school councils.

---

[2] Alice Miel, *Changing the Curriculum* (New York: Appleton-Century-Crofts, Inc., 1946), p. 64.

Third, there is the system level. Such representative or composite groups of status leadership as may be designated are responsible for planning general policies concerning the programs of all the schools for effecting desired learnings. Representative councils, departmental and grade groups, special committees, individuals or groups having particular interests, and sometimes the whole group may carry on this planning, with the legal responsible body, the board of education, having final responsibility. There may be a hierarchy of planning groups at this level; that is the local district may need to work out plans consistent with those of the county school authorities and the county with those of the state. All these plans may be affected by state laws and regulations of the state board of education, as described in Chapter 3.

Fourth, there is a level we may classify as external. Although having no legal or administrative relationship to the school, an accrediting association may have considerable influence on local curriculum planning. Through research studies and publications and curriculum materials, professional associations frequently contribute very directly to local planning groups. Also, curriculum planning which affects local groups indirectly but sometimes quite forcibly is done by various organized groups throughout the nation who seek to influence what is taught in school in relation to their interests. They may work through direct publications and speakers and films for schools, or through pressure on legislatures, boards, school curriculum planning groups, and textbook writers. Although the processes of curriculum planning are fundamentally the same at each level, it is important to keep these distinctions in mind since the nature of participation is somewhat different from level to level.[3]

Essentials of organization. Essential to organization are (a) some form of council or coordinating committee, (b) task forces such as ad hoc or standing committees, and (c) key staff to relate the organizational structure back to administrative units and also to service the committees as they work. Loosely organized committees without tasks, deadlines and services are merely shams. Curriculum development is a necessary function of educational administration and must meet the demands placed upon it.

The Role of the State and the Nation

The role of the state. Given semi-autonomous districts, what is the role of the state? As has been indicated, it reserves some powers and states some conditions. It cannot give resources and authority

---

[3] J. Galen Saylor and William M. Alexander, *Curriculum Planning* (New York: Holt, Rinehart & Winston, Inc., © 1954), pp. 538–539.

to a municipal creature which does not function. Hence it must set some general conditions of operation. For instance, it can require that a twelve-month program be operated, or that all children be served in terms of their needs, or that teachers have tenure and be certificated. If it wants the last full measure of efficiency, however, it must set up wise instructional policies that:

1. Encourage and put a premium on increasing the variation and scope of local programs.
2. Encourage research, experimentation and evaluation.
3. Carry on cooperative research programs.
4. Provide political and psychological support to local curriculum development.
5. Provide for and administer a cooperative state curriculum program.
6. Provide consultative services through specialized personnel—personnel specialized in the processes of curriculum and/or the uncommon problems in education.
7. Provide the needed financial resources.

As to process it is important that a great deal of cooperative planning and action take place at all times. Fixed roles do not contribute a great deal to a cooperative venture so emphasis is placed on communication and cooperation as well as on function, structure and role.

In most states an intermediate district with more or less autonomy enters into curriculum development, but the pattern varies greatly. *The principles of curriculum development that apply to truly local community units apply to the county district* if it is the only local school district as in Florida or West Virginia. Generally the difficulties of implementation are greater in the county district than in the community district. More and more studies are being made designed to work out the best methods of operation in county districts. When an intermediate unit of some kind is interposed between the local district and the state, such as an administrative or supervisory district, it is certain to have a negative or confusing effect unless its service role is carefully planned in relation to the roles of the local district and the state.

The role of the nation. The role of the nation in curriculum development is a moot one. What kind and amount of curriculum development is needed in a centralized nation? In a federated nation? Centralized nations are taking a serious view of these matters. The United Kingdom and the Union of Socialist Soviet Republics are two nations taking serious action in this respect. In such countries educational reform dealing with broad public policy issues such as scope of program takes precedence over more detailed problems of content and method. The national role as it finally emerges in federal systems must be based on a clear and correctly defined concept of the role of the state.

Organization and services at the national level. The greatly increased federal role in educational affairs has been discussed. The practical problem of organization at the federal level must be faced. The Office of Education has a history of weakness brought about by design. The responsibilities of that Office have, however, been increasing steadily and in spite of its submerged position. From a small statistical bureau with nominal leadership in education it has grown to a large organization. Curriculum leadership functions have steadily increased. Little can be said about the future except that its future will certainly be very different from its past. The need arises for an agency to which will be assigned a quite independent role. Insofar as curriculum development is concerned the need is for a bureau which will be concerned with research and planning at the federal level, research leadership which will permeate the various communities and states, democratic curriculum planning with emphasis on pointing out urgent curriculum needs and increasing communication about curriculum developments. Lastly, such an office should maintain liaison and provide services to the vast number of agencies that provide national leadership in instructional affairs.

Control functions and democratic leadership functions should be sharply differentiated within the national office. Curriculum leadership should be obvious enough and emphatic enough to present a functional organization concerned with improving instruction rather than one concerned with inhibiting or disorganizing curriculum developments through specious grants-in-aid, legal mandates and inevitable audits.

Organization of the Local District

The problem of organization for curriculum development in a local school district is an interesting technical problem. Much attention has been given to the matter and the literature is replete with references. Organization for getting a function carried out cannot be thought of as being of one pattern. Organization must conform to certain values and principles but it can vary tremendously and still achieve its purposes. Experience has shown that morale and functional efficiency are high when certain favorable conditions exist.

The importance, nature and criteria for organization have already been set forth earlier in this chapter. In setting up an organization several issues must be faced.

First of all, entire school systems must be involved in the organization. The chief administrative officer must occupy himself engrossingly with the organization and must see that principal officers are deeply involved. In other words, curriculum development cannot be effectively departmentalized or delegated. Departmentalization and delegation tend to fragmentize the educational program unnecessarily, to weaken the support given to a given curriculum area and to encourage isolation and obsolescence. Departmentalization and delegation tend to separate the part from the whole, e.g., from the high school program as a whole or the science program as a whole or the twelfth grade program as a whole.

A second issue has to do with representation. Representation should be broad and inclusive. The school principals alone, the headquarters staff alone, or both together, or teachers alone make an ineffective curriculum council or an ineffective task force. Some curriculum councils have good teacher and administrative representatives but no parent, school board member, pupil, business, labor or agriculture representatives. It can be readily seen that a local curriculum workshop made up of 600 teachers and 100 parent leaders is infinitely more effective than a workshop made up of teachers only when it comes to getting local support for curriculum change.

In the same way a curriculum council which consists of administrators, teachers, citizens and learners is more powerful than a narrowly-based council.

Representation has many ramifications and if pushed too far can be objectionable by itself. So in determining representation much attention must be given to the reasons for representation, to the possibilities of meaningful involvement, and to the dangers of meaningless representation. The negative aspects can be avoided by good planning and good organization. For instance, a curriculum council can be made up of panels of students, teachers and citizens. These panels can meet singly or jointly as the tasks might require.

Thirdly, the organization should lead to a maximal amount of *production* and *communication*. This consideration warns against accumulating just "so many bodies." It suggests that people be accepted or assigned according to their ability to contribute to the solution of some problem.

Fourthly, organization should be flexible and changeable. Since there is nothing fundamental about organization it should be subject to scrutiny at all times. If it gets in the way of progress it should be changed or abolished. The criteria and capability for evaluating the organization should be built into the administrative scheme.

McNally, Passow and their associates have made available seven excellent program descriptions.[5] These descriptions illustrate the kinds of organizations utilized in a state program of instructional improvement, two county programs and four local district programs. These examples illustrate some of the organizational principles and forms that may be used and are fairly typical of the better curriculum development programs in the country. The critiques included in the seven chapters are especially illuminating.

Since there is nothing very fixed about organization most educators are prone to think that existing line and staff as well as less formal organizations are quite adequate. This is a fallacy as demonstrated by the entire research and development movement of modern times. The inherent resistance to change and the travail that goes into the finding of any new solution are so great that only the cleverest organization, only the wisest use of staff, and only the sagest leadership can overcome obsolescence.

Roles of specialized staff. The specialized staff of a school system consists of line administrators, curriculum specialists and numerous other people with special assignments who are there to make teaching possible. The primary specialist, the teacher, is a special case and will be considered later.

All specialized staff have roles to play in curriculm development but these staff members are so numerous and different as to defy treatment except to say that they will find their tasks in any good cooperative program.

The curriculum specialist is, of course, of central importance. Confusion about his role stems from two principal sources. His role has evolved out of the role of the supervisor to a very large extent and the supervisor traditionally was more concerned with curriculum control and conformity in method than with growth and development. The second source was the prevalence of authoritarian administrative practices. Out of this background developed the concept of a specialist in learning, in individual therapy and in

---

[5] Harold J. McNally, A. Harry Passow, and Associates, *Improving the Quality of Public School Programs* (New York: Bureau of Publications, Teachers College, Columbia University, 1960).

group leadership using unique skills in a democratic setting. Naturally, such a drastic change in theory has come about slowly and practices usually do not conform closely to the theory. But the direction is firmly established.

A typical local organization. The confused situation at the local level is shown in Chart A below. While no two school districts agree on organization, Chart A is fairly typical of a vast number of large school districts who have added specialists to the staff of the chief administrative officer as the curriculum became extended and as coordination of the curriculum development activity increased in difficulty and urgency.

Chart A scarcely gives a hint of the hundreds of curriculum development activities and the nature of the process that goes on in the school system. It is clear, however, that the organization is friendlier to departmental rigidity than it is to cooperative planning and action.

CHART A

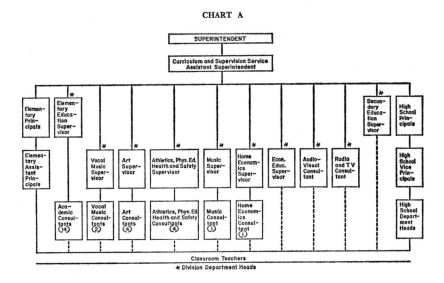

Trends in Organization

Trends in organization are difficult to pinpoint when reduced to the problem of curriculum development. Recent emphases in educational administration have been particularly noticeable, such as the interpersonal setting, the human relations concept, the emphasis on the informal versus the formal line and staff organization and the use of councils and committees. Many of these new emphases grew out of experimental efforts to improve instruction.

The problem of coordination. Education is seeking for a democratic solution to the problem of administrative coordination. The best guess is to create a plan in which instructional improvement remains the principal concern of the chief administrative officer and at the same time adequate and competent manpower is available to coordinate and encourage instructional improvement. Research, staff growth and curriculum planning are coordinated under one individual or council. Departmentalization of instructional improvement activities into one or several departments is avoided. Various organizational solutions are being tried out such as an overall coordinator for small school districts or an associate superintendent in charge of instruction for large school districts.

The roles of various curriculum technicians. As for curriculum workers in general, there is a real trend toward assigning all curriculum specialists to consultative roles. In a consultative role a specialist has an opportunity to achieve good rapport with other professionals, to concentrate on the use of his peculiar skills and to be freed from petty administrative tasks. The trend is to use more and more specialists to help teachers and to further research and development. Rather than moving toward fewer specialists of the same kind, that is, experts in processes of curriculum development, school districts are increasing the variety of specialists as well as the number. For instance, specialists in language and science are being utilized as consultants, but all such specialists are becoming specialized in curriculum process also. While the first emphasis in departmental curriculum projects is usually on subject matter problems such as internal integration of subject matter and sequence, inevitably such problems as relationships with other departments or subject matters, teacher efficiency, teaching method, teaching materials, curriculum planning, diffusion of innovating practices, and evaluation soon claim the attention of staff members. These problems are all embraced in the process of curriculum development. In dealing with the second group of problems the specialist soon discovers that he is a curriculum specialist.

The need for curriculum change is so great that a few staff specialists cannot meet it. In a well-organized program general administrators, teachers, counselors, personnel directors, nurses, psychometricians and all other kinds of auxiliary personnel are involved in curriculum development. Sometimes the role is very minor. Maybe only data on need are given by health personnel, maybe only help in scheduling is given by a general administrator, but the participation is necessary and important. A good example is the trend to give a teacher of mathematics extended re-education in subject matter and method and then to make him available as a helping teacher on a part-time or full-time basis.

In addition to the staff people in a local district every learner, parent, citizen, hobbyist and technician in the community is used as a resource person in an effective curriculum project. A centenarian may make a tape on local history, a medical man may authenticate the content in a health unit or a trade unionist may explain the objectives of his organization. In effect, each local district has a pool of resource persons of its own and it uses this pool to improve instruction as well as to carry out routine processes.

The curriculum specialists or technicians in the various types of school systems have a great variety of titles and assignments. The developing situation as to roles and titles are such that assigned roles and titles vary so much that they are practically meaningless. Usually the higher ranking titles such as "assistant superintendent" and "supervisor" imply more administrative and coordinative functions than titles like "helping teacher" or "consultant." But still this generalization cannot be depended on.

Looking at the roles of these agents from a competency point of view it can be said that allowing for degree of competency curriculum technicians should have and do have at least considerable competency in (a) school organization and administration, (b) human development and learning, (c) social conditions as they affect the school, (d) scholarship in subject matter, (e) group processes, (f) helping teachers to identify and solve their problems, (g) instructional materials, (h) evaluation and educational research. Implicit in the role is the obligation to grow in all of these areas.

The Utilization of Outside Resources

Since the local school district, and its community, are a small part of a greater whole it must reach out to build and validate its curriculum. The resources of the state, the university and the world are available. These resources are being greatly expanded. Nearly every university now has a field service. States are augmenting consultative services. State and federal agencies produce more and more educational materials. Educational foundations are increasing their funds and planning resources. Social and economic agencies are increasingly accepting education as an indispensable instrumentality and are cooperating with educational agencies.

The professional organizations to which teachers belong represent powerful resource agencies. These range from the general organization to the host of special organizations based on a broad area of subject matter, a discipline, or on a process such as administration or research.

The effective local program uses all of these resources in the implementation of its program of research, staff growth and curriculum development.

The Central Role of the Teacher

It is in the teacher's role that all curriculum development is focussed. Not only does the teacher participate in developing new teaching-learning procedures but it is the teacher who is the principal consumer of innovations in the field of education. Since all good teaching is creative and artistic to a considerable degree the teacher must adapt or validate the new procedure for himself. This fact points the way to a close relationship between curriculum development and the in-service education of teachers.

Participation of all kinds of resource people, leadership and commitment by the administration, spade-work by the curriculum specialist are all important but the role of the teacher is basic. The teacher must have the desire to change, must be a party to the formulation and adoption of the curriculum policy, must participate in developing new plans and procedures and must put the new procedure to the test. No partial participation is effective. Because of this the best curriculum programs in states and exceptionally large school districts can never be fully efficient unless decentralized. For the same reasons decentralization is important even in a small district.

Services for Curriculum Development

Some of the services for curriculum development are built into the typical situation. Administration as service as well as administration as a directing force is a good example and needs little discussion. Logistics such as buildings, transportation and the like are illustrations of services.

Services that loom up as important are personnel services provided by part-time and full-time personnel such as consultants. As has been indicated more and more services by specialized personnel are needed and provided as education faces the problem of expanding needs and improved quality. The quantity and nature of services from specialized personnel is expanding rapidly. All state departments of education, as well as the Office of Education, are annually increasing staff and services. Institutions of higher education are increasing service staff and services. Most significant of all is the rapid increase of supervisors, consultants, helping teachers, special teachers, coordinators and assistant superintendents at the school district level.

Publications as an important service. A part of the work of curriculum specialists is the preparation of curriculum guides and instructional materials. Often the curriculum specialist only coordinates and edits such publications drawing on the work of teachers, laymen and other specialists for much of the developmental work and writing. The great bulk of instructional materials comes from the commercial publishers who provide an inestimable service. They in turn, however, are guided to some extent by curriculum specialists. Curriculum guides are being developed by the thousands at all times in local school districts. Some of these become available to the profession.

The Office of Education publishes certain curriculum guides as well as research studies. Illustrations of these are the following:

Elementary School Organization—What Direction Shall It Take
High School Pupil Programs
The Junior High School
Programs for the Educationally Disadvantaged
Offering and Enrollments
Non-graded Schools
Team Teaching in the Elementary School

In addition to studies and guides the Office of Education publishes the administrative regulations for many congressional acts most of which contain curriculum guides of a mandatory or near-mandatory nature which have great influence on curriculum development.

The Association for Supervision and Curriculum Development publishes annually a listing of materials exhibited at their annual conference. This listing[6] is useful to curriculum workers and pro-

---

[6] Association for Supervision and Curriculum Development, *Curriculum Materials 1965* (Washington, D.C.: The Association, 1965).

vides a representative sample of the kinds of curriculum materials being prepared.

The National Education Association prepares and distributes a wide variety of curriculum materials. An examination of one of their catalogs[7] shows how the various studies and affiliated organizations that operate under the aegis of the N.E.A. produce everything from bibliographies to filmstrips on almost every conceivable educational problem. Some of these publications have to do with the professional purposes of the organization but most of them are guide materials which help solve curriculum problems and increase communication nationally.

Publications in the local school district.   All medium and large school districts publish materials as a part of administrative process. These include mimeographed directions; very valid types of instructional materials such as local histories; research reports and curriculum guides containing the curriculum plans in current use.

The local district depends a great deal on the publications available from outside sources.

The curriculum center as a service.   The curriculum development activity being relatively new has suffered from poor administration and logistics. Apart from the problem of organization is the problem of functionally planned space and money for supplies, equipment and travel.

The curriculum specialist equipped only with a desk and a telephone is as archaic as a farmer with a hoe. A curriculum center which is a distribution center for books and audio-visual equipment, a technical library on curriculum development and magazines represents a real need of a good curriculum program. Even vending machines for food and drink are essentials in a fast-moving effective program since every effort should be made to increase the effectiveness of groups of people who can only be brought together with considerable effort. Curriculum centers of various kinds exist in medium and large school districts.

---

[7] National Education Association, *Publications Catalog 1964–1965* (Washington, D.C.: The Association, 1965).

CHAPTER VI

Curriculum Development As
In-Service Education

In-service education, curriculum development and supervision are recognized by all authorities as being closely related concepts. Each concept borrows from the other two when defined or discussed separately. Articles and books on in-service education generally refer to curriculum development and supervision as vehicles. In the same manner discussions of curriculum development and supervision tend to refer to in-service education as merely a method or an adjunct.

When curriculum development is seen as a broad and comprehensive program of school administration it is not difficult to see that it embraces supervision and in-service education. When, in addition, the theory of curriculum development assumes (a) that the chief purpose of all educational administration is the improvement of instruction and (b) that curriculum development deals principally with the creative re-education of the teacher, the three concepts and programs fall into place. To some people the concept of supervision is not needed and is considered obsolete and even objectionable. But what is more important is the fact that all three concepts are logically, meaningfully and closely related if the central objective of instructional improvement is kept in mind and used as the principal criterion.

Participation of the teacher in learning to improve his practices amounts to a creative re-education of the teacher. This is the impact of Zirbes book[1] previously referred to. George Sharp stated the essential assumption and defended it in his book entitled *Curriculum Development As Re-Education of the Teacher*.[2]

This assumption about purpose has been inherent in every good curriculum development program whenever curriculum development has replaced curriculum revision and whenever creative demo-

---

[1] Laura Zirbes, *Spurs to Creative Teaching* (New York: G. P. Putnam's Sons, 1950), pp. 90–91.

[2] George Sharp, *Curriculum Development As Re-Education of the Teacher* (New York: Teachers College, Bureau of Publications, Columbia University, 1951).

cratic leadership has replaced an administrative and supervisory control of instruction aimed at conformity.

The need, scope and methods of the in-service education of teachers are well summarized by Moffitt who stresses change and states that:

> With all that has been written and discussed about continuous expansions and alterations of the curriculum, it must be understood that the curriculum changes only as the teacher changes it.[3]

Emphasis on the role of the teacher in curriculum development does not mean that the growth of other staff members is not important as well. Administrators and service personnel have essentially the same growth needs in relation to their roles as do teachers. Nor does emphasizing the importance of the teacher negate the importance of research results, new overall curriculum plans or new teaching-learning procedures. These are all important products but they do not come first or stand alone. When school systems maintain good communication and coordination the curriculum development process through careful planning and evaluation keeps the total program in reasonable balance.

The large subject of in-service education in all of its aspects was treated by the National Society for the Study of Education in its Fifty-Sixth Yearbook, Part I.[4] This volume is quite eclectic and was published during the formative period of in-service education programs. It outlines the scope, relationships and importance of in-service education as an instrumentality. It led to more extensive and to more definitive thinking by the profession. Much of this thinking is summarized in the *Encyclopedia of Educational Research.*[5]

Implications for Personnel Policy

The integral relationship that exists between curriculum development and staff growth has brought about changes in personnel policy. Local administration usually builds into its personnel policies, promotional plans and pay schedules and other provisions designed to favor staff growth. Premiums are placed upon research, experi-

---

[3] John Clifton Moffitt, *In-Service Education for Teachers* (New York: The Center for Applied Research in Education, Inc., 1963), p. 12.

[4] National Society for the Study of Education, *In-Service Education for Teachers, Supervisors and Administrators,* Fifty-Sixth Yearbook, Part I (Chicago: University of Chicago Press, 1957).

[5] Chester W. Harris, ed., *The Encyclopedia of Educational Research,* 3rd ed., (New York: MacMillan Co., 1960).

mentation and advanced study. Even the routine obligations of teachers are often defined in such a way as to require direct contributions to leadership, planning and research.

Without the support of good personnel policies curriculum development loses much of its initiative and effectiveness.

Inseparabilty of a school improvement program. While the program of in-service education is broad it can be readily seen that the curriculum development program is inseparable from it. In a real sense all other parts of the school improvement program are auxiliary to the curriculum development program since educational administration exists to bring about program improvement through new learning opportunities and through improved teaching-learning procedures.

The implication that grows out of the concept of relatedness is that the administration will provide for the joint planning of all administrative services under its aegis. Rather than thinking of in-service education and curriculum development as unrelated entities, it is better to think of them as the Siamese twins of a total program of instructional improvement. Only with a cooperative program based on the most careful planning of all elements in the educational institution and its entire community or constituency can the pitfalls of departmentalization and duplication be avoided. Good planning is creative in nature. It opens up avenues for self-expression for individuals and at the same time disciplines and supports each individual and agency concerned.

A Concerted Administrative Effort

In Chapter V the importance of a concerted administrative effort was discussed. In considering the role of in-service education it is necessary to come back to the concept of totality. Probably in-service education and pupil personnel services are the two important functions most frequently departmentalized to the detriment of the school system. The solution is not to put everything under the caption of curriculum development but rather to keep all related activities in close relationship. Attempts to maintain this relationship through careful structuring alone usually fail. There exists, to the contrary, a general consensus on the desirability of flexible, continuous, cooperative planning and evaluation.

Illustrations of good curriculum programs. In one of the best analyses of desirable programs of curriculum development[6] the authors approach curriculum development as an entirety—as a broad system-wide effort. An examination of the seven case studies contained in chapters 5–11 shows clearly how in-service education functions in a school system dedicated to continuous curriculum development. Professional courses, faculty meetings, administrative council meetings, travel, research, experimentation, writing, committee-work, learning to use teaching aids, viewing films, restating goals, revising programs in such areas as reading, science and mathematics, role playing, keeping diaries, inventorying community resources, carrying out new group guidance activities, organizing youth seminars are a few of the in-service education activities. *Because of the global nature of these school improvement programs these activities are truly curriculum development activities.* And so the twain have ever met under good administrative leadership! And so also do guidance services, in-service education and supervision meld into a total program when a total school improvement program exists.

Unfortunately, while the seven programs described and analyzed by McNally, Passow and Associates like those reported in the predecessor volume[7] could be matched by a hundred more, these programs represent more or less the consensus as to what practice should be but not the norm of school practices as they exist in all school systems.

Another report on in-service programs. Spears[8] pulled together a number of case studies of in-service education which could as well be called case studies of curriculum development. His estimate that in-service education programs when loosely defined could be considered to be practically universal agrees with other studies. He generalizes on his examples by stating eight principles or propositions:

1. The professional training of the teacher does not cease as he leaves the college for the teaching position.
2. Nor can his future professional development be adequately served by continuous teaching experience alone.

---

[6] Harold J. McNally, A. Harry Passow and Associates, *Improving the Quality of Public School Programs* (New York: Bureau of Publications, Teachers College, Columbia University, 1960).

[7] Hollis L. Caswell and Associates, *Curriculum Improvement in Public School Systems* (New York: Bureau of Publications, Teachers College, Columbia University, 1950).

[8] Harold Spears, *Curriculum Planning Through In-Service Programs* (Englewood Cliffs, N.J.: Prentice-Hall, Inc., © 1951), pp. 315–316.

3. Although it is reasonable to expect a teacher to guide his own future development, it is the obligation of the school system to stimulate the advancement of its staff by providing opportunities for teachers to grow on the job.
4. These opportunities when properly planned and coordinated can be called the in-service education program of that school district.
5. The provision of staff leadership for this program is a legitimate school expenditure.
6. The test of the in-service program lies in the improvement of the instruction and, consequently, in the improved development of the pupils.
7. The in-service program cannot be separated either in spirit or function from curriculum planning and supervision, the three representing overlapping features of the program for instructional improvement.
8. Although the prime purpose of in-service training is to promote the continuous growth of teachers, a portion of the effort represents the elimination of deficiencies of those who were inadequately trained during their pre-service education. For instance, it was recently reported that 32 per cent of the elementary-school classroom teachers and 3 per cent of the secondary-school classroom teachers of the country had less than four years of college preparation.

Three Directions for In-Service Education

An examination of development and practice suggests three directions for in-service education—one might say future directions except that all three are already recognized to some extent. These directions are (a) adhering to the central criterion, (b) emphasizing creative re-education of the educational worker whatever his role, and (c) emphasizing self-study of the professional.

Adhering to the central criterion. The improvement of the total program of an institution in terms of the extent and quality of services gives in-service education a stern criterion if properly applied. This criterion suggests the exclusion of purely personal or professional activities. Further, it prevents the setting up of programs that are purposeless. The criterion *cannot* be adhered to unless a mechanism and a process of overall planning and evaluation exists in a given educational institution and unless that mechanism and process represents the *alter ego* of the administration which is here intended to mean the decision-making operation of the institution. The administration composes not only the chief administrative officer but the board of control, the profession and other groups such as learners, parents and electors.

In large establishments formal research studies of need and efficiency are definitely implied.

Emphasizing creative re-education of staff. The concept of curriculum development as re-education has already been discussed in this chapter. But studies of practice do not indicate any wide use of the idea. In fact, many recent developments such as television teaching, the use of teaching machines and even team teaching have, perhaps inadvertently, tended rather to move away from creative re-education of staff members.

The need is to keep the emphasis on creative re-education regardless of the teaching situation. Beggs has proposed a new model for the teacher.[9] His proposed abilities—the ability to achieve synthesis, the ability to coordinate and the ability to serve as a catalyst—suggests that teaching and re-education of teachers leave much room for creativity. While the proposal is novel it is not necessarily inimical to the idea of creative re-education anymore than is team teaching.

Nor should the emphasis on creativity be thought of in connection with teachers alone. Administrators should be creative too. The American Association of School Administrators recognizes the need for in-service education for administrators. In a 1963 report[10] the entire gamut of in-service programs is dealt with in a very general manner. The organization sustains an in-service program for administrators and seeks to refine and extend it. Such a program should emphasize creative re-education since administration should be one of the most creative human activities but it is too often thought of as restraining the good things in life.

Emphasizing self study of the professional. Jersild[11] has focussed attention on the self-study approach and shown the depth of that approach. Recent developments in psychology and psychiatric therapy suggest the dangers of treating professionals *en masse.* They also suggest the folly of driving teachers to master a given technique when the crying need of such teachers might be much deeper in nature. The nature of basic personal problems such as loss of status in his own circle should be considered in formulating in-service education programs. The seriousness of anxieties and the role of

[9] Walter K. Beggs, *The Education of Teachers* (New York: The Center for Applied Research in Education, Inc., 1965), pp. 196–197.

[10] American Association of School Administrators, *In-Service Education for School Administrators* (Washington, D.C.: The Association, 1963).

[11] Arthur T. Jersild, *When Teachers Face Themselves* (New York: Bureau of Publications, Teachers College, Columbia University, 1955).

anxiety in both its positive and negative valences need to be considered.

The self-study approach is not new. It was recognized early in the development of supervision. The future development of in-service education should include a new look at basic threats to mental health and should seek new ways of meeting deeper personal needs of professionals as well as professional needs such as mastering a new teaching method. Psychology should be put to work as a tool The possibilities of affective learning should be fully exploited.

CHAPTER VII

Newer Practices in
Curriculum Development

Against the background of the history and nature of curriculum development it is possible to consider newer practices with considerable perspective. In examining newer practices it should be borne in mind that they originated in real situations because of the presence of significant needs, forces and perceptions.

The importance of newer practices may be due to an intensification of effort as illustrated by attempts to create a new and better program for teaching science. Other practices are important because they represent attempts to use education to implement socio-educational goals as illustrated by newer practices in vocational education, in increasing the holding power of secondary schools, in strengthening economics education and in bringing education to under-privileged groups. Some of the newer practices are important largely for methodological reasons, for example, team teaching and the utilization of the newer technology of education such as television teaching and programmed learning. Other newer practices have more specious but no less significant implications.

The Environment for the Newer Practices

The newer practices that were reported in the curriculum literature of 1935–1940 operated in a climate or a society which has been rather thoroughly discussed in Chapter II. The emphasis then was on social and curricular change, on a burgeoning democratic society, on utilizing the best in educational philosophy and research in the classroom.

The environment of the space age period which includes the social and educational forces at play is quite different. Nowhere were the implications of atomic fission and space travel more influential than in education and especially in curriculum and method. The actual norm of classroom practice probably changed little but experimental efforts were nevertheless very influential. These experimental efforts grew out of a dissatisfaction with the old. There developed a tendency to break with the past and ignore the long lines of educational development. Earlier concerns like the integration of subject matter, making instruction relate to personal problems of learners, and improving the emotional environment of the learner were to a very great extent ignored by those concerned with programmed learning, television teaching, intellectualization of curriculum and twelve-year sequences for the subject matters.

The background of the theoretical thinking about instruction is well illustrated in *Theories of Instruction*.[1] In this document are papers dealing with curriculum, instruction, teaching and learning. These papers which represent clear thinking and writing when considered separately also demonstrate an increase in the level of confusion when taken as a whole. For one thing the papers tend to ignore the larger boundaries of the educational process as well as to imply invalid and unrealistic differences between the four aspects of the education process—curriculum, instruction, teaching and learning. Furthermore, the emphasis on learning and the learner which increased gradually and considerably from 1920–1940 is largely supplanted by the emphasis on control by the administration, the teacher or the teaching device. These are major issues.

The final paper by Walcott H. Beatty deals with some of the basic issues raised by the various theoretical propositions in the other papers. Beatty's statement of the issue of "shaping" versus "choice-making" provides a fundamental criterion for the interpretation and evaluation of the newer practices in education. He feels that an education that "shapes" an individual through planned teaching-learning procedures will produce an individual somewhat incapacitated to live in the kind of free society we seem to cherish and that teaching-learning procedures that lead to choice-making will produce a healthy, confident individual capable of living richly and creatively in the free societies of the upcoming century.

Looking at Newer Practices Critically

As has been indicated, the newer practices in education are important because they represent change and experimentation. Taken as an aggregate they provide the evidence for the actual trends in education. Taken separately they provide the experimenter with a

---

[1] Association for Supervision and Curriculum Development, *Theories of Instruction* (Washington, D.C.: The Association, 1965).

fount of experience from which he can design his experiment and save valuable time and effort otherwise wasted in trial and error.

One way to examine a new practice is to treat it as an interesting phenomenon. It is always interesting to see how any idea is planned and carried out. Critical observation, however, must be based on certain assumptions used as criteria. Numerous sets of criteria have been developed. One of the best and most usable since it has been employed in an actual investigation is that found in *Improving the Quality of Public School Programs.*[2] Few specialists would disagree seriously with the criteria or with their scope. They provide a useful instrument for evaluating case studies of total programs or singular developments.

These forty-four criteria which deal with the dimensions of program improvement are grouped under the following concepts: scope and objectives, initiating program improvement activities, administration, organization, procedures and techniques and evaluation.

Use of democratic principles and group processes. As has been shown curriculum development because of its cooperative nature is dependent on the application of democratic principles to school administration. While John Dewey[3] had pointed out repeatedly the unique relationship existing between democracy as a concept or ideal and education as a function during the first two decades of the twentieth century it was not until the third decade that experimentation and reporting occurred. *Democracy in School Administration,*[4] which has been referred to, provided a statement covering rationale and practices in 1943. By this time group processes had been explored in the fields of psychology and sociology but had been little used in education. Actually, the wide application of group processes to school administration and particularly to in-service education of teachers and to curriculum development came after World War II.

Any cursory review of the literature of curriculum development will reveal that where there are serious attempts at curriculum development group processes are widely used even though authoritarian administration may also be present in some degree. Group

---

[2] Harold J. McNally, A. Harry Passow and Associates, *Improving the Quality of Public School Programs* (New York: Bureau of Publications, Teachers College, Columbia University, 1960), Chap. XII, pp. 311–320.

[3] John Dewey, *Democracy in Education* (New York: The Macmillan Co., 1916).

[4] G. Robert Koopman, Paul J. Misner and Alice M. Miel, *Democracy in School Administration* (New York: Appleton-Century-Crofts, Inc., 1943).

processes have been generally accepted and are widely used in nearly all human endeavors.

Local and state curriculum programs do generally use group processes in a framework of democratic administration. Such processes are used for a variety of purposes, principal among which are the following:

1. Evaluating existing instructional programs
2. Evaluating the curriculum development program itself
3. Helping staff members to develop a feeling of need for change
4. Obtaining consensuses on educational objectives
5. Planning and conducting conferences
6. Planning and conducting research studies
7. Enhancing communication
8. Conducting committee work
9. Conducting in-service education activities
10. Pupil-teacher planning in the classroom.

The core curriculum method illustrates an important and comprehensive use of group processes in elementary and secondary school classrooms. This method is carefully explained and illustrated by Faunce and Bossing.[5] The utilization of this method at the adult level is vividly developed by Kelley in his book[6] on workshop method.

The core curriculum method represents a rather perfect model for curriculum development on a microcosmic basis. It is a method, often referred to as a general method, for implementing or developing the curriculum in a given school or school system. The method is usually employed in the common or required segment of a curriculum although the dynamic process of teacher-pupil planning can be used in any situation. Many practitioners feel that the objectives of general education can be better attained when the curriculum is built around the common needs problems and interests of learners. Alberty[7] feels that the method should be used in a framework of established problem areas. In actual practice the programming is usually related and confined to certain subject matter areas. In either case, the curriculum, or experience unit, is made on the spot. The teacher (or teachers), learners, resource people, parents, represen-

---

[5] Roland C. Faunce and Nelson L. Bossing, *Developing the Core Curriculum* (Englewood Cliffs, N.J.: Prentice-Hall, Inc., 1951).

[6] Earl C. Kelley, *The Workshop Way of Learning* (New York: Harper & Row, Publishers, 1951).

[7] Harold Alberty, *Reorganizing the High School Curriculum* (New York: The Macmillan Co., 1953), pp. 178–180.

tatives of social agencies, and interested citizens are all involved. General direction is provided by the curriculum plan and general objectives of the school authority just as it is under the traditional unit. Specific educational objectives, however, having to do both with ways of behaving in relation to others and control of subject matter are derived and accepted by the group process. Teaching-learning procedures are cooperatively planned and executed. Evaluative data are collected, organized and interpreted by the group process in terms of all objectives.

The self-contained classroom at the elementary school level, a very significant new practice, utilizes the same general method of teaching and curriculum development in an even more extensive manner[8] than does the care curriculum method.

It can be readily seen that this method of teaching has great value for the development of staff, for learning to use group process and for curriculum development in general. It provides a complete learning laboratory for all concerned.

As in other complex situations, evaluations are not entirely conclusive. Not only are data difficult to secure and organize but also the values and perceptions of those doing the evaluating play a very important part. Smith who takes the position that ". . . group processes are an important and useful resource as teaching brings about changes in individual pupil behavior"[9] explains the way the process is utilized in the classroom in a small pamphlet.

Wide Participation of All Concerned

Based on the principles fundamental to group process but approached and valued separately is the method of wide participation. Such participation represents a distinct break with the procedures of the past. More and more students, parents, publishers, social agency personnel, school staff members, school board members, members of legislatures, and citizens in general are asked to participate in curriculum development.

Involvement of learners. Students are involved in curriculum development through participation in student council planning, through membership on curriculum committees and through

---

[8] Association for Supervision and Curriculum Development, *The Self-Contained Classroom* (Washington, D.C.: The Association, 1959).

[9] Louis M. Smith, *Group Processes in Elementary and Secondary Schools,* National Education Association, Department of Classroom Teachers and the American Educational Research Association (Washington, D.C.: 1959).

teacher-pupil planning of classroom activities. Parents, aunts, uncles and grandparents help to plan and service neighborhood school programs. Citizens of all imaginable categories serve on curriculum committees, neighborhood school councils, school building planning committees, and fund raising committees. In these roles they contribute by helping to determine policy and contribute financial resources at one extreme and to serve coffee at the other extreme.

Involvement of school board members. School board members are citizens with a very special role in education. Their participation in curriculum affairs is extensive. The role of local boards of education in curriculum development is extremely significant. Boards of control that are removed from the community, such as intermediate school district and state school district boards, may concentrate on hearing evidence and making policy decisions. Local boards of education, however, must operate within the community and at the same time maintain their ability to separate the policy making role from the participatory role. Certainly school board members must avoid the mistake of administering the educational program while at the same time they assure themselves of its adequacy. Tuttle[10] treats the matter rather fully. He concludes that:

> The time is clearly at hand for each board to concentrate its attention on the curriculum to make certain that its educational program does in fact "meet the stern demands of the era we are entering," as emphasized by the President of the United States. At the same time, it should neither be the desire nor the intention of the board to assume any professional administrative responsibility in curriculum matters.

> Following are some of the ways that have been used by boards to build their own background of understanding as to what the schools shall teach, and to enlist the cooperation of both professional educators and the general public in developing and maintaining the best possible curriculum policies:
>
> 1. Schedule board meetings so as to devote at least as much time to curriculum matters as to business affairs. This may be accomplished either by dividing the time at each meeting, or by holding alternate meetings for the two purposes.
> 2. Send out agenda to board members well in advance of meetings so that they may have time for study and understanding as a basis for consideration.

10 Reproduced from *School Board Leadership in America,* 1963 Edition, by special permission of the author and copyright owner, Edward Mowbray Tuttle, pp. 76–78.

3. Streamline board meetings to conserve time spent on details and increase opportunities for educational discussion.

4. Request the superintendent to arrange with his staff to have various phases of the educational program presented to the board by directors of instruction, teachers, principals, and others at successive board meetings, until all of the courses of study in the curriculum are clearly understood by the board members.

5. Where feasible, hold board meetings at different schools in the system so that the members may become better acquainted with the work of all the schools.

6. Provide the means for securing on the instructional staff the best qualified and most competent teachers that can be found, as the surest way of guaranteeing that the established curriculum will be carried out effectively.

7. Make certain that the superintendent of schools is not overwhelmed with routine work that could just as well be done by business and clerical assistants to free his time for study, supervision, and evaluation of the educational program, which is his major responsibility.

8. Ask the superintendent to report frequently and exactly as to how well particular courses in the curriculum are working out in terms of the desired objectives, with recommendations for any indicated modifications of policy.

9. Look upon the evaluation and modification of curriculum policies as a continuous process of harmonious evolution, rather than as a subject for occasional study with resulting periodic upheavals.

10. Enlist the aid of community groups and committees in studies of various kinds with respect to how well certain courses in the school program are meeting the wishes and desires of the people in the community, and what extension or curtailment of the curriculum may be indicated (see Chapter 17).

11. Support members of the teaching staff unequivocally in their presentation of facts concerning controversial issues, provided only that sincere effort is always made to present such facts objectively and impartially.

12. Agree upon a generous policy toward providing the quantity and quality of instructional materials recommended by teachers to enable them to present the established courses in the curriculum most effectively.

13. Spend as much time as possible individually reading books, periodicals, reports from the superintendent, and other materials relating to curriculum matters, to provide background for informed discussion in board meetings and in public contacts.

14. Attend district, state, regional, and national meetings of

board members and other groups where school curriculum problems will be discussed and ideas exchanged.

15. Secure, whenever conditions seem to require it, the advice and counsel of professional educators and consultants from colleges, universities, and state departments of education, who will meet with the board and superintendent to explain new ideas and concepts of instruction and curriculum planning.

Participation through the community school.   Ernest Melby in speaking of participation in the Flint (Michigan) Community Schools says: "I have never known a person who came to play a real part in a school system, who contributed of his mind and heart to the enterprise and who didn't support it. Over and over again we see people who have had little or no interest in education. They become involved in the school system. They come in and give talks and participate in curriculum committees. They help with bond issue campaigns. They give of themselves in many ways and from then on they are solid supporters of education. If we are ever to convince the American people of the need for a more dynamic educational system, we will do it as we lead people to more active participation."[11]

Participation rests on a theory which is in the formative stage. In the simplest sense it is based on the *democratic concept of equality* of individuals and the idea of getting everybody into the act. In the community school movement the theory is more profound as has already been indicated. The concept of inventorying and meeting all needs, the idea of the comprehensive educational program and the belief in a program responsive to community and individual needs make special demands on participation.

The operation of the community school is based on as extensive involvement of all individuals and agencies in the community as possible. Everyone is a participant or is entitled to participation in the same sense as he is a member of the community. The community school goes even further and assumes that everyone in the world appertains in some possible way and is a potential resource. The community school is a complete system of participation but so too, in a sense, is any fully developed state or local curriculum development program.

Cooperative planning of school plants.   The need for new school plants following World War II provided the dynamics and

---

[11] Ernest O. Melby, "Keynote to the Theme, a Report of the First National Community School Clinic," *The Journal of Educational Sociology,* XXIII, No. 4, (1959).

resources for much excellent curriculum planning. Some school authorities, either with the aid of educational foundations and universities or with their own resources, set up long-range research-based programs. Dearborn, Michigan was an early example. In this case local resources were augmented by university and foundation funds. Lower Merion Township in Ardmore, Pennsylvania used primarily its own resources; Morrilton in Arkansas had its resources augmented by foundation funds; Kanawha County in West Virginia teamed up with a university;[12] Melbourne, Florida gained much help from foundation funds. But in all cases need and local initiative were the driving forces.

More important than the outstanding projects were the hundreds of school districts which involved all categories of community personnel in planning for new school buildings throughout the country —notably in states where initiative was left to communities by the state education authority.

The outstanding characteristics of the movement can be summarized as follows:

1. Extensive curriculum planning designed to envision an educational program based on educational needs and purposes.

    The result is a statement called educational specifications which served as a basis for physical planning.
2. Considerable participation by other categories of personnel than administrators, architects, financiers and contractors. The participation often includes prospective learners, parents, teachers and community leaders.
3. The utilization of new ideas obtained through reading, travel, group discussion and listening to experts brought into the community.
4. Planning of each specific school building or facility in terms of the long-range needs of the community.

    This trend brought about in many cases a level of planning dealing with a specific building and a broader level dealing with system-wide educational needs, plans and facilities.
5. Lastly and probably most important is utilization of the process of group thinking and rationalization in terms of purposes, means and plant plans.

Curriculum development was greatly expanded and enhanced by such cooperative and thorough planning for new facilities.

---

12 *Toward Self-Direction* (Columbus, Ohio: Bureau of Educational Research and Service, The Ohio State University, 1962).

Work of Heavily Endowed Curriculum Commissions

The rash of unrest and criticism that followed the successful launching of the first space vehicle, Sputnik I, brought about the motivation and organization of some approaches in depth through heavily endowed studies of education and curriculum development projects. The studies, such as those headed by James Bryant Conant, were rather cursory in nature but still influential. They served to turn the attention of professionals and laymen to educational needs and weaknesses. Their constructive influence was not great but they stimulated thinking and brought about subsequent inquiries and experiments. They also brought about an emphasis on the need for quality.

The curriculum commissions which set up continuing programs have been more influential than the studies. These commissions, such as those organized to deal with such key fields as physical sciences, biological sciences, foreign languages, economics and mathematics brought the disciplines back into the curriculum field. They encouraged and continue to encourage the participation of people who are highly competent as scholars in an organized field of subject matter. They bring financial resources as well. Lastly, they help to deal with subject matter obsolescence brought about by the prodigious changes in the amount and nature of findings in any given field. Traditionally, school curriculums grew out of the organized disciplines. Curriculum workers and those who produce teaching aids organize knowledge into teaching packages. But obsolescence creeps in as time passes. The obsolescence expresses itself not only in subject matter but also in the competency of the teacher, in curriculum policy, and in teaching materials.

One of the most beneficial effects of the subject-centered commissions has been their influence on teacher education. In the institutions of higher education greater emphasis has been put on the role of subject matter departments in the preparation of teachers. Professional groups such as the American Association for the Advancement of Science and various professional organizations such as chemical and engineering societies have supported teacher education very strongly.

Scope of the subject matter movement. The enthusiasts for the subject matter curriculum development projects feel that they constitute *the* reform movement. Actually, they represent a significant aspect of the total continuing effort to develop an effective curriculum for the American school. An excellent report on the various projects was produced by Goodlad in 1964.[13] While additional projects are appearing such as the industrial arts project, the scope is shown in the appendix which lists the following:

1. *Mathematics*
   University of Illinois Committee on School Mathematics
   1208 West Springfield, Urbana, Illinois;
   School Mathematics Study Group
   Stanford University, Stanford, California;
   University of Maryland Mathematics Project
   College of Education, College Park, Maryland;
   Experimental Project in the Teaching of Elementary-School
      Mathematics
   Stanford University, Stanford, California;
   University of Illinois Arithmetic Project
   University of Illinois, Urbana, Illinois;
   The Greater Cleveland Mathematics Program
   Educational Research Council of Greater Cleveland
   75 Public Square, Cleveland, Ohio;
   The Syracuse University-Webster College Madison Project
   The Madison Project, Syracuse, New York;
   Geometry Project of the Department of Mathematics of Stan-
      ford University
   Stanford University, Stanford, California.

2. *Physics*
   Physical Science Study Committee
   Educational Services Inv., 164 Main St., Watertown,
      Massachusetts.

3. *Biology*
   Biological Sciences Curriculum Study
   University of Colorado, Boulder, Colorado.

4. *Chemistry*
   Chemical Bond Approach Project
   Earlham College, Richmond, Indiana;
   Chemical Education Materials Study
   University of California, Berkeley, California.

5. *Elementary School Science*
   Elementary-School Science Project
   University of Illinois, 805 W. Pennsylvania Ave., Urbana,
      Illinois;
   Elementary-School Science Project
   University of California, Berkeley, California;

---

[13] John I. Goodlad, *School Curriculum Reform in the United States* (New York: The Fund for the Advancement of Education, 1964).

Science—A Process Approach
American Association for the Advancement of Science
1515 Massachusetts Avenue, N.W., Washington, D.C.

6. *Science*

The Science Curriculum: K-12 Approach
National Science Teachers Association, 1201-17th Street, N.W.,
 Washington, D.C.;
Science Curriculum Program of the Science Manpower Project
Teachers College, Columbia University, New York, New York;
The Elementary Science Study
Educational Services Inc.
164 Main Street, Watertown, Massachusetts.

7. *Social Sciences*

High School Geography Project
1785 Massachusetts Avenue, N.W., Washington, D.C.;
Anthropology Curriculum Study Project
5632 Kimbark Avenue, Chicago, Illinois;
Project Social Studies
Cooperative Research Program, Office of Education, U.S. De-
 partment of Health, Education and Welfare, Washington, D.C.;
Greater Cleveland Social Science Program
Educational Research Council of Greater Cleveland
Rockefeller Building, Cleveland, Ohio;
Elkhart Indiana Experiment in Economic Education
Department of Economics, Purdue University, West Lafayette,
 Indiana.

8. *English*

Commission on English, 687 Boylston Street, Boston, Massachusetts;
Project English
Cooperative Research Program, Office of Education, U.S. Department of Health, Education and Welfare, Washington, D.C.

9. *Foreign Languages*

Foreign Language Program of the Modern Language Association of America
70 Fifth Avenue, New York, New York;
A-L-M Audio-Lingual Materials: French, German, Italian, Rus-
 sian, Spanish
Modern Language Materials Development Center
2 East 20th Street, New York, New York.

These projects represent a considerable effort and they exert a
great influence on curriculum development in this country and
abroad. Some of the results such as updating of subject matter are

of permanent value but the schematic aspects such as sequence and teaching methods must still stand the test of time.

The Association for Supervision and Curriculum Development has presented a broader treatment of curriculum development by way of the subject matter approach and includes vocational education as a curriculum area. This volume deals with ". . . Trends, emphases, problems and assessments of curriculum development work in the fields of the arts, English, foreign languages, health education and physical education, mathematics, science, social studies, vocational education and instructional technology are presented. The authors have not only reported on the current curriculum developments but have made a case for change and have pointed out the problems and prospects ahead."[14]

Weaknesses of the subject matter projects.　The subject matter oriented curriculum commissions have a disruptive influence in that they are naturally concerned with only one part of the curriculum but then it is the business of the duly constituted school district, state or other authority, to insure balance and meaningfulness to an educational program. School systems having strong curriculum development programs have accepted the challenge and brought in the new emphases without serious loss of balance in the curriculum. Unfortunately most school systems have not had the creative, specialized personnel with which to make these adjustments.

The various projects tend to ignore the needs of non-college going students and to ignore certain important educational objectives. Alexander and Michael state these criticisms as follows:

> Further curriculum studies must dig harder to find a content, possibly far removed from the time-honored disciplines, which makes more of a dent on the child who comes to school disinterested and unmotivated in subjects he perceives as frozen in a way of life that all too frequently is not for him. And even more privileged youth, including those strongly motivated for higher education, need school opportunities which will help them achieve competencies in addition to those required for college success in specialization in the disciplines.

> Partially because of these neglected objectives, continuing curriculum study must involve the development of more comprehensive curriculum models. These models must begin with the total spectrum of school objectives rather than with the separate disciplines, and hypothesize ways of using new subject matter of the old sub-

---

[14] Association for Supervision and Curriculum Development, *New Curriculum Developments* (Washington, D.C.: The Association, 1965), Foreword, p. vi.

jects and from whatever other sources content can be drawn, to achieve these objectives. Furthermore, these models should be seen in actual school operation, that is, in experimental schools established for this purpose rather than just in papers and charts of curriculum theory, useful as the latter may be. There may be no more promising way of advancing American education than the establishment and long-term operation of publicly supported educational centers organized and conducted to try out in full detail the most complete and hopefully adequate curriculum models we can design. Schools allied with these centers may be able to develop curriculum plans that lead rather than lag.[15]

Other weaknesses of the projects are over-emphasis on the production of instructional materials, lack of adjustment to the nature of the learner and planning subject matter content from the top down. In his Section III, Conclusions and Recommendations, Goodlad[16] has made a clear analysis of difficulties and stated clearly his recommendations for strengthening the projects. Many of the weaknesses of the projects could be cared for by following these recommendations.

Lastly it must be recognized that most of the curriculum projects are basically "throw-backs" to the era of curriculum revision. Many teachers and curriculum specialists find it obnoxious to use an approach with the basic weaknesses characteristic of most of the projects. The compensatory aspects of the projects such as adequate resources and the support of scholars, of industry and key community leaders are recognized as offsetting advantages.

An example of the subject matter approach.   Actually the disciplinary groups often represent fairly broad fields and involve many related agencies. They are bound together by a common cause. In the case of the economic education movement economists, business leaders, teachers, labor organizations, union leaders, representatives of governmental agencies and private business corporations as well as a host of others joined together to increase economic literacy. Many approaches were used. Organizations were formed, existing organizations agreed to assume certain cooperative roles, money was raised and the general public was well informed of an important educational need.

In the early stages leadership and resources were brought to bear on an extensive workshop program for experienced teachers and

---

[15] Association for Supervision and Curriculum Development, *New Curriculum Developments* (Washington, D.C.: The Association, 1965), p. 101.

[16] John I. Goodlad, *School Curriculum Reform in the United States* (New York: The Fund for the Advancement of Education, 1964).

administrators which reached into nearly every state and into hundreds of schools. To this as a principal approach was then added a curriculum approach called the Developmental Economic Education Program.[17] Under this program millions of learners, thousands of teachers and hundreds of communities are joined in a massive effort. Research, preparation of curriculum materials, new offerings in teacher education, educational testing, filmed lessons and the usual curriculum development methods are employed.

In the case of the workshop and the curriculum project the teaching of economics is strengthened and increased. Moreover, the movement embraces many other subject matter fields. It includes a general emphasis on citizenship and even exceeds the boundaries of a broad field approach. The movement is fully described by Frankel[18] in a definitive volume.

Likewise the emphasis on more and better science teaching or foreign language teaching spills over into other fields and into curriculum experimentation and teacher education.

Programs Developed under National Legislative Grants-in-Aid

The urgency and importance of rapid curriculum change was recognized by the U.S. Congress by the establishment of national grants-in-aid to states, school districts, colleges and individuals. The precedent for this action existed in the post-Civil War grants to institutions of higher education and the post-World War I grants to teacher educating institutions and states for the support of vocational education.

The first National Defense Education Act was designed principally to improve the quality and scope of the teaching of science, mathematics and the foreign languages. Grants-in-aid for educational research were also made available under another act and then followed aid to other subject matter areas. The Congress also funded the National Science Foundation which concerned itself with the improvement of science education.

The National Defense Education Act had very significant implications for curriculum development and significant changes were

---

[17] James D. Calderwood, *Teachers Guide to Developmental Economic Education Project,* Part One (New York: Joint Council of Economic Education, 1964).

[18] M. L. Frankel, *Economic Education* (New York: The Center for Applied Research in Education, Inc., 1965).

made in local school systems as a result. In spite of the specious nature of the aid, most school systems made improvements in the scope and quality of their programs of science, mathematics and foreign language teaching. Guidance as an implementary service was also strengthened. In systems having good instructional leadership excellent curriculum plans were put into operation and the federal support was used to supplement an on-going program of curriculum improvement. In many local situations, however, the result was merely more emphasis on the subject matters receiving federal support.

Fighting poverty with education. The attempt to eliminate pockets of poverty in the U.S.A. utilized education as an instrument in many ways. Education received support from the anti-poverty legislation on the one hand, such as the Economic Opportunity Acts, and from educational legislation such as the expanded aid to vocational education and the Elementary and Secondary Education Act of 1965. All of this legislation created new or expanded educational programs and new problems and opportunities for curriculum development. Jobless young people were given sustenance and education in special schools with especially designed curriculums and methods. Vocational education programs were expanded to care for more of the occupational needs of young people. Children of nursery school or kindergarten age were given special instruction in "head-start" programs designed to overcome lack of educational privileges and to create a readiness for participation in regular day school activities with other children.

The Elementary and Secondary Education Act of 1965 was primarily supportive in nature and designed to further the anti-poverty program. It did, however, add to the fermenting curriculum situation by strengthening budgets of local schools and by a number of specific provisions. Notable among these provisions were those under Title III which made grants available for the support of supplementary educational centers and services designed to stimulate and assist in the provision of vitally needed educational services not otherwise available and to stimulate and assist in the development and establishment of exemplary educational programs to serve as models for regular school programs. It is obvious that the planning of such new centers and services would cause any school system or technician to rethink existing situations and to attempt to create experimental situations designed to bring about better education.

Implications of recent federal legislation. The most obvious implications of the recent federal legislation seem to be the following: (1) federal support has assumed massive proportions making the federal government a partner in all public education and some non-public education, (2) many of the provisions present curriculum workers with new opportunities for significant curriculum development, and (3) the large issue of federal control was left outstanding in the first batch of significant federal educational legislation since the early acts initiating vocational education following World War I. Educational philosophers and curriculum specialists maintain a very wary stance but the position of most administrators seems to be that expressed by Superintendent Shedd:

> How can federal resources best be utilized by curriculum workers? Curriculum workers would include all persons who have a responsibility for children and young people within the schools. Teachers, principals, curriculum specialists, guidance personnel, psychologists and superintendents are all curriculum workers.
>
> Many readers have already made use of NDEA funds for improving curriculum in science, foreign languages and for improving guidance services, which funds have been available since 1958. This act was amended, expanded and extended through the enactment of the National Education Improvement Act of 1963, but the procedures for utilizing these resources in special areas were retained pretty much as before.
>
> What about the newer legislation, which has more far-reaching and even revolutionary implications for public school systems, the Economic Opportunity Act, and the new Elementary and Secondary Education Act of 1965? Both of these acts call for new approaches within the school and in relation to the community. Both are looking to local community leadership to have the imagination, creativity and commitment to be serious about improving and equalizing educational opportunity. The money will be available but not until educators are willing to provide the leadership. Here, I believe, is the real challenge to curriculum workers. If we are not equipped to accept this challenge, someone else will do our job for us.[19]

Galen Saylor's[20] position, on the other hand, is representative of many specialists in curriculum and general administrators. While making a strong case for federal participation in educational affairs Saylor fears "the stifling of the creativeness, inventiveness, and skill of discovery" of local educational leaders and officials as well as the

[19] Mark R. Shedd, "The Federal Colossus in Education—Curriculum Planning," *Educational Leadership*, XXIII, No. 1, October 1965, pp. 15–16.

[20] Galen Saylor, "The Federal Colossus in Education—Threat or Promise?" *Educational Leadership*, XXIII, No. 1, October 1965, pp. 7–14.

"invidious control over the program of education itself." In terms of extension of bureaucratic control he warns against national testing programs and a change in the basic cultural attitudes of people to the extent that they might adopt the passive attitudes characteristic of the European and other older cultures accustomed to bureacratic control. As has been indicated earlier the trend to develop bold and creative educational patterns that developed between 1920 and 1960 might well be sharply revised and curriculum development might be superseded by servile adjustments to administrative and legislative mandates.

The extent to which federal intervention will become a threat or a promise remains to be seen.[21] The highest educational authority, for instance, denied the intention of the government to institute a national testing program. How Congress will act in arming the executive branch with controls cannot be predicted although at this writing recent legislative acts have greatly extended federal controls. The tendency of a bureau to exert controls can, however, be fairly and well judged by referring to history. American, as well as older cultures, attest to the tendency of bureaus to extend controls over-zealously unless restrained by powerful cultural and constitutional conditions.

The actions of the Congress were the principal nationalizing influences after 1958. These actions plus the influences of certain non-public agencies had an immediate effect on the schools—both good and bad. Some of the principal results were the following:

1. Courses and programs in science, mathematics and foreign languages were substantially changed.
2. The advanced placement program under which secondary school students could earn college credit spread rapidly.
3. Guidance programs in secondary schools were greatly increased and changed.
4. Testing programs originated and largely controlled by agencies outside of the schools were vastly extended.
5. A new pattern of in-service education of teachers was established in the form of federally financed institutes.
6. Federal funds made available curriculum materials and teaching aids not previously procurable by many poorer school districts.

Curriculum workers welcomed the leadership and resources released by federal appropriations and educational foundations. They

[21] Roald F. Campbell and Robert A. Bunnell, *Nationalizing Influences on Secondary Education* (Chicago: Midwest Administration Center, The University of Chicago, 1963).

recognized that federal intervention exposed the lack of initiative and flexibility on the part of local and state authorities. They took advantage of the reaction to these exposures by increasing the scope of curriculum development and the rate of curriculum change. While recognizing the responsibility of the operating unit or local district to keep the balance in education they deplored the mandatory nature of the externally imposed programs and the extension of rigid administrative controls in the field of instructional policy and practice.

Use of Curriculum Development in Attacking Social Problems

The curriculum development approach to the solution of social problems is not new but note must be taken of several projects in this area which are momentous and new. Besides the anti-poverty effort two additional examples of the conscious use of curriculum development to attack social problems stand out.

The Great Cities Project. The Great Cities project represents an attempt in fourteen of our largest cities to use curriculum development, research, an amassment of resources and a new school program to deal with the difficult situation that has developed in the core of most great American cities. These cities have received foundation support which was later augmented by federal support. Focussing on the culturally deprived children in these urban situations the curriculum workers, social workers, researchers have looked at the whole child, at the family and the unique social situation. With the situation analyzed in this way the school as a dynamic agency, with increased resources, with a new and better oriented staff has produced a new and enriched program of school services ranging from better, richer instructional services to more and better social services. The effect has been a limited community school program.

This experiment showed what could be done.[22] It remains to be seen whether or not the new practices will be supported with public funds on a continuous basis. In a very real sense it served as a precursor to several educational aspects of the anti-poverty program.

The Holding Power Project. The vexing unemployment prob-

---

[22] U.S. Department of Health, Education, and Welfare, Office of Education, Bulletin 1963, No. 17, *Program for the Educationally Disadvantaged* (Washington, D.C.: United States Government Printing Office, 1963).

lem and the presence of youth in secondary schools which do not meet their needs has led to systematic attempts to hold youth in school and to give them a worthwhile program while attending school. Some states have organized school holding power projects. These developments led to a nationwide holding power project which is broadening the approach. This project is still in a devlopmental stage at this writing but it is an excellent example of the use of curriculum development and research in dealing with a deep, complex and fundamental social problem. This approach like that of the Great Cities Project enlists public interest and support on a broad basis and leads to a simultaneous attack on social, economic, racial and programming problems. It has also received support from state and federal departments of government other than education.

The International-Intercultural Education Emphasis

Kaleidoscopic developments in world affairs have led to a sharp increase in international-intercultural education activities. Not only the federal government but a host of international and educational organizations have contributed to the movement. The North Central Association of Schools and Colleges led the way with a very impactful educational project at the secondary education level. This Project dealt not only with curriculum development but also prepared and experimented with new teaching materials.

An experiment in Glens Falls, New York demonstrated the curricular possibilities at the community level. This project is reported in the Glens Falls Story.[23]

Much international intercultural education has dealt with the United Nations.[24] A government bulletin dealing with this subject shows the scope of this aspect of international intercultural education.

The Community School Movement

The most comprehensive and practical attempt to bring about curriculum development in a cultural context is found in the community school movement. It represents a synthesis of all efforts to

---

[23] National Council for the Social Studies, *Improving the Teaching of World Affairs—The Glens Falls Story*, Bulletin No. 35 (Washington, D.C.: The Council, 1964).

[24] U.S. Department of Health, Education, and Welfare, Office of Education, Bulletin No. 18, *Teaching About the United Nations* (Washington, D.C.: The U.S. Government Printing Office, 1960).

bring about meaningful curriculum change. Thus one finds in Flint (Michigan), Miami (Florida) or in any good community school development simultaneous attacks on holding power, international understanding, poverty and many other social problems. The community school movement has its own curriculum theory, indicated in Chapter I, which fits into a total program for serving individual needs and thus bringing about an ever-improving community. The unique and extensive use of group processes and citizen participation is described elsewhere in this chapter.

Use of the New Methods Approach

The most controversial of the newer practices is what can best be called the "new methods" approach. This approach has been openly espoused by many individuals and by one major foundation. The trend is based on the assumption that there is a new, known technology that can increase the efficiency of education immensely. Great emphasis has been placed on the new technological developments such as the use of television and teaching machines. Stress has also been placed on using teacher aides, on better organization of the secondary school program, on cooperative teams of teachers and on greater use of educational tests. Supported by foundation funds the trend has had considerable impact.

Quite properly some specialists insist on the importance of "programmed instruction"[25] where the emphasis is on a "program" which leads the learner through a set of specified experiences designed to help him reach a specified objective or objectives. This new emphasis on the "program" is an improvement on the textbook and workbook, both forms of programmed instruction, because it makes use of many new techniques such as teaching machines and audio-visual aids.

So far all evaluations are tentative and it is impossible to generalize very much on the broad effects. Many evaluations have dealt only with the success of specific projects and thus the results are specious rather than general. The controversiality of the movement has been salutary in that it has caused a re-examination of the weaknesses of education and an examination of new teaching-learning procedures.

Team teaching as a technique. Cooperative teaching is as old

[25] Wilbur Schramm, *Programmed Instruction* (New York: The Fund for the Advancement of Education, 1962).

as departmentalization and as strong as the plan and individuals involved. The term refers to many practices. The self-contained classroom served by a homeroom teacher and many resource people is one well-defined practice. A more recent practice generally referred to as a part of the new methods approach is the cooperative teaching unit that uses a definite hierarchy of personnel such as the "master teacher" aided by teachers with special skills, non-professional teacher aids and often teaching interns who are primarily trainees. Some schemes bring together the skills of teachers in the same department only while others bring about a sort of integration by teaming teachers from different departments. The most ambitious of the schemes is the school-within-a-school or the "suite" or "wing" idea. This plan is often developed as a new school facility is planned which raises serious questions about flexibility or inflexibility should education change significantly in future years.

> The heart of the concept of team teaching lies not in details of structure and organization but more in the essential spirit of cooperative planning, constant collaboration, close unity, unrestrained communication, and sincere sharing. It is reflected not in a group of individuals articulating together but rather in a group which is a single, unified team. Inherent in the plan is an increased degree of flexibility for teacher responsibility, grouping policies and practices, and size of groups and an invigorating spirit of freedom and opportunity to revamp programs to meet the educational needs of children. In a sense it might be said that the proponents of the movement question administrative and organizational restrictions of the past and hold that school administration exists primarily as a service medium, not as a control function.[26]

Generally speaking, team teaching at this time of writing is considered to be a promising experiment which must vary from school level to school level. The principle of cooperation is not considered to be controversial. Other aspects are definitely experimental in nature.

Ungrading the graded school. The desirability of ungrading graded schools has long been recognized since it is related to the goal of adjusting instruction to individual differences. Much experimentation appeared in the period following World War II and no counter trend has developed. By 1965 over half of the large school

---

[26] Stuart E. Dean, "Team Teaching in the Elementary School," *Education Briefs,* No. 38 (Washington, D.C.: Office of Education, U.S. Department of Health, Education and Welfare, January 1962).

systems in the U.S.A. had ungraded some grades of schools.[27] Most of the ungraded practices are found at the elementary school level and especially in the kindergarten and the first three grades. Sporadic and piece-meal experiments are found at all levels and in some school systems extensive changes have taken place.

Ungrading secondary schools has taken place to some extent with beneficial results. At this level ungrading takes place usually in the required or general education area. The problem of ungrading is quite different in the elementary and secondary school levels because the system of unit credits used in secondary schools traditionally has provided a technique of ungraded that has been utilized very skillfully in many secondary schools.

Dufay[28] surveyed ungraded elementary schools and found many advantages such as elimination of the retention or grade failure problem and the acceleration problem for the span of years included in the ungraded block; better socialization due to "inter-age mixing," a practice explored years before in secondary schools; better achievement in reading skills; and several administrative advantages such as better use of teacher skills, better use of facilities and unique and desirable forms of reporting to parents, and flexible scheduling.

Like many other innovations ungrading schools can be mismanaged. Teachers who have learned to care for individual differences in self-contained classrooms which are well supplied with a team of specialists and with modern teaching aids may find few advantages and many disadvantages in ungrading. The most serious weakness is the over-use or wrong use of grouping which is already prevalent in American elementary schools. If the young child is used as a pawn in a game of control of subject matter the growth of the child is inevitably threatened. Fortunately the experiments in ungrading are also very favorable to the right use of grouping and other forms of individualization of instruction.

The ungraded experiments fit quite well into the "new methods" approach since they encourage the use of the new technology of teaching and call attention to the manner of instructing individuals more than groups.

27 National Education Association, *Nongraded Schools,* Research Memo 65–12 (Washington, D.C.: The Association, May 1965).
28 Frank R. Dufay, *Ungrading the Elementary School* (West Nyack, N.Y.: Parker Publishing Company, 1965).

Publications on Current Developments

One way to determine new developments is to note the titles of current publications. The Association for Supervision and Curriculum Development has published books and booklets on many current educational problems. Their choices indicate developments at a given time in an objective manner.

Yearbooks

1. Role of Supervisor and Curriculum Director in a Climate of Change (1965)
2. Individualizing Instruction (1964)
3. New Insights and the Curriculum (1963)
4. Perceiving, Behaving, Becoming: A New Focus for Education (1962)
5. Balance in the Curriculum (1961)
6. Leadership for Improving Instruction (1960)
7. Learning and the Teacher (1959)
8. A Look at Continuity in the School Program (1958)

Booklets

1. Changing Curriculum Content
2. Children's Social Learning: Implications of Research and Expert Study
3. Criteria for Curriculum Decisions in Teacher Education
4. Developing Programs for Young Adolescents
5. Discipline for Today's Children and Youth
6. Educating for Economic Competence
7. Elementary School Science: Research, Theory and Practice
8. Extending the School Year
9. Foreign Language Teaching in Elementary Schools: An Examination of Current Practices
10. Freeing Capacity To Learn
11. The High School We Need
12. Human Variability and Learning
13. Improving Language Arts Instruction Through Research
14. Intellectual Development: Another Look
15. The Junior High School We Need
16. The Junior High School We Saw
17. Juvenile Delinquency: Research, Theory and Comment
18. Labels and Fingerprints
19. Learning More About Learning
20. New Dimensions in Learning
21. Nurturing Individual Potential
22. The Self-Contained Classroom
23. Supervision in Action

24. Teaching Music in the Elementary Schools: Opinion and Comment
25. The Three R's in the Elementary School
26. Trial and Error in the Improvement of Education
27. Using Current Curriculum Developments
28. What Are the Sources of the Curriculum? A Symposium.

These titles help define the nature of curriculum development. Of course, hundreds of other commercial and professional agencies also publish curriculum materials—some for the commercial field designed to meet a recognized need for instructional aids and some designed to carry out the purposes of the associated groups.

Newer Practices Are Legion

It is impossible to give a fair picture of newer practices in education even if reference is confined to only a couple of decades. There are hundreds of categories and thousands of examples. Economic education can be matched by equally important related developments in conservation education and outdoor education. Newer developments in health education which are extensive and can be said to include the burgeoning field of driver education have not been mentioned. Creative education which is considered by many to have a unique importance in an automated society has not been treated. The education of exceptional children which expanded tremendously between 1950–1965 and which has included talented individuals as well as individuals with special deficiencies has developed many new curricular practices. Every new practice brings significant implications for curriculum development.

CHAPTER VIII

The Great Issues in
Curriculum Development

About fifty years of curriculum development and ten years of tough educational debate sparked by the launching of Sputnik I have brought education to a significant turning point. This turning point will probably carry the date established by the Eighty-Ninth Congress when it passed the Elementary and Secondary Education Act of 1965. This Act has certain curricular implications but more than that it signals the assumption of responsibility for the daily, on-going fiscal support of public education by the federal government. Once the federal tax dollar is put behind average operating costs of education to the extent of about twenty per cent, once the federal government assumes responsibility for equalizing educational opportunities and once the federal government decides to determine emphases in curriculum and method, it will almost certainly continue until the federal role is fairly well defined.

Certain issues seem to be very important in the sense of priority in the sense that a given decision on these issues will determine educational direction for the future. The issues discussed herein seem incontestably to be *great* issues but they may be no more important than certain other issues better presented and better supported. Possibly they should be described as key issues. At any rate, the following issues must be dealt with in a positive and forthright manner if progress is to be maximized.

The first two issues are basic to curriculum development but are essentially public policy issues fundamental to the nature of education and to curriculum development in a free society. The other three issues are, primarily, educational or technical policies but are also public policies of general import. These are:

Issue   I—What shall be the public policy on the role of education?
Issue   II—What shall be the public policy on centralization of educational administration?
Issue III—What shall be the educational policy on the role and nature of curriculum development and staff growth?

Issue IV—What shall be the role of research and development in
      education?

Issue V—What shall be the roles of curriculum specialists and
      related personnel?

These issues all have many significant implications of a general
nature but they will be discussed, primarily, from the point of view
of curriculum development.

Their significance can be appreciated if one takes from history
cases where certain policies were adopted and acted upon. There
are many such precedents. The decision to make education primarily
a public function rather than a private or clerical function is an illus-
tration in the field of public policy. In the field of curriculum the
variation in practice of curriculum control and development in the
fifty American states is classic. New York has clearly demonstrated
the results of a strong, well-supported centralized system in a highly
developed culture. Hawaii and Alaska are laboratories where the
effects of centralized state systems may be observed in unique situations only recently removed from the territorial status. Michigan
and other states carved out of the Northwest Territory have demonstrated the effects on instructional efficiency of little state centralization and much local freedom.

Only the imagination aided by some comparative thinking can
help envision the possible and probable results of using research and
research results as a basis for curriculum development with a minimum of retardation due to the fetters of tradition and external
controls.

Great Issues in Curriculum Development

Public policy on the role of education.   Issue I—What is to be
the role of education?

In a given society, be it a community, political subdivision, or
nation, which of four or more solutions shall be chosen? Shall education be considered an agent of the national political system to be
used pragmatically to prepare certain categories of personnel and to
purvey national political propaganda of a one-party system? This
was tried out in Germany and Italy under the dictators. It is still
being demonstrated in several nations with totalitarian regimes.

Or—shall education be recognized as an important function but
administered on a laissez-faire basis with more or less public aid but
no direction as to purpose except that inherent in the culture? This

policy is quite common and has a long history. Many new nations rely on this policy today. Many American states rely on this policy.

Or—shall education be considered to be an important state function to which the state gives good support, strong control and forceful leadership? This policy is in force in numerous states and nations.

Or—shall education be considered to be of *prime* importance, the prerequisite to cultural development and survival? As such education would be given as high a priority on public resources as would risk capital or defense. This solution would lead to the use of education as an instrument for coping with both personal and public problems such as the orientation and development of a delinquent child or the large problems of poverty, unemployment and defense.

Under this option curriculum development would be constant, continuous and creative. Likewise education would increase categorically, quantitatively and in quality because the support would be available as would the personal and public resources. Already the tendency to adopt this last type of public policy is apparent in several countries, including the U.S.A., but no breakthrough has really appeared.

Under a positive public policy curriculum development would merge with broad administrative program planning very smoothly and effectively.

Public policy on the degree and nature of centralization. Issue II—To what extent shall education be centralized and in what fashion?

A certain amount of centralization is inherent in the organization which is characteristic of any society or governmental organization. Education being a major function, government must assign responsibility for its administration. Responsibility, embracing as it does control, evaluation and support, implies a certain amount of centralization. The real question is whether centralization shall be intentionally, as a matter of policy, maximized or minimized. To maximize centralization is to increase controls and to minimize variation, individual responsibility, initiative, creative curriculum planning and the meeting of new and unusual needs. To centralize is also to minimize the differences inherent in the sub-cultures of communities, political subdivisions, and regions within a given jurisdiction be it a city, county, province, state or region containing various states or other units.

The concepts of centralization and decentralization are not two opposite demons in this situation. The genius of any solution lies in careful selection of the role of authority—a central authority source always exists in political systems.

The questions at issue are (a) how much power to fixate in basic statutes, (b) how to use the power, including the question of how little may be used without endangering the operation (sometimes referred to as the Jeffersonian "law of parsimony," and (b) what powers of review should be insisted on by the delegating authority.

Experience indicates clearly (a) that with strong centralization there is no curriculum development as such, (b) that traditional needs are met rather well but that new needs are perceived and met only in a tardy and cumbersome manner, (c) that staff growth is stultified and (d) that the resources and initiative of the individual citizen are little used. Further it seems clear from the history of dictatorships that when centralization is dictatorial neither truth nor efficiency can be found. On the other hand it seems clear that decentralization tends to increase the general interest of everyone in curriculum development, challenges curriculum specialists and makes potential curriculum workers out of almost everyone.

The increased concern and intervention of national authorities in the curriculum field as evidenced by the National Defense Education Act should be a signal for an all-out re-examination of the principles underlying centralization and decentralization. There is plenty of evidence to show that any increase in bureaucracy in a culture, no matter how honest, brings about a decrease in references to the individual conscience, to research and to unbiased professional opinion. True, many large organizations do develop institutional practices to overcome the hazards of centralization—and to good effect. Some examples are research departments, leadership development programs and in-service education programs. These are good practices but the question is that of determining precisely the point at which further centralization is undesirable.

Finally, it must be recognized that the objections to across-the-board decentralization should not lead to weakening of responsibility or inaction by the highest authority. If the role of education is to be enhanced, the central authorities must be *concerned and influential.* They must be judicious in their intervention and seek to stimulate and enhance rather than hinder individual and local initiative. They must also respect and enlarge the role of the community, school or college as a social entity and organization. They must seek to enhance the professional worker and the education profession. Enhancement of the roles of all agents leads to progress. Diminution of roles tends to lead to stagnation and regression.

Decentralization without positive democratic leadership obviously has no merit from an administrative point of view. At its best *laissez faire* leadership has led to a few very creative developments but these can be matched by many more examples of chaotic and slipshod situations which have led many people to support strong centralized systems. The case for a positive but democratic form of educational leadership is made rather forcefully by Campbell and his associates in *Practical Applications of Democratic Administration*[1] and by Weber and Weber in *Fundamentals of Educational Leadership*.[2]

Educational policy on curriculum development and staff growth. Issue III—Shall program development through curriculum development and staff growth be made the central purpose and activity of educational administration?

This issue is of such great social importance that it would seem erroneous to label it a technical issue. In fact, it is the prime issue any member of a board of control of an educational institution should have in mind. But it is, in a sense, an internal issue. To decide in favor of program improvement and staff improvement means to alter the working roles of everyone. It means more curriculum specialists. It means that curriculum specialists will be doing creative work rather than performing routine tasks as is often the case. To vote against continuous program is to assume that any educational program of services is adequate, that a curriculum pattern can be considered to be firmly established and that staff skills do not suffer from serious obsolescence. It even assumes that staff morale and efficiency can be maintained at a given level in a static organization —something that has never been proved even in the best managed establishments.

There may be a tendency to belabor this issue but in the many developmental studies carried on since 1935 it has been difficult to find a majority of selected schools and school districts that would maintain a general commitment to curriculum change and staff growth. The cultural norm is based on the idea that a good school has a good program and executes it fairly well—with no break-

---

[1] Clyde M. Campbell, *et al., Practical Applications of Democratic Administration* (New York: Harper and Row, Publishers, 1952).

[2] C. A. Weber and Mary E. Weber, *Fundamentals of Educational Leadership* (New York: McGraw-Hill Book Co., 1955).

downs. The need for drastic improvements in holding power, in method and in curriculum is not generally felt. Nor is the idea of a new expanded education a part of the cultural aspiration.

Critics, both friendly and unfriendly, know that tradition, quietude, and low performance are the rule and that alertness in curriculum development and aggressiveness in regard to staff growth are the exception rather than the rule. Without a commitment and a process to carry it out, obsolescence of both program and staff is inevitable in a changing culture in which invention and change are as certain and swift as the passage of time.

Stress must be placed on the policy of curriculum development because without policy the process is weakened and the best individual professionals are rendered inept and useless and even placed in jeopardy. This is waste.

Policy on research and development. Issue IV—Shall research and development be accepted in education?

Research and the application of research findings have been explored in education but application on a broad scale has not yet been accepted. Research institutions are rare in education compared with medicine. Research items in public education budgets are the exception although Congress has made a good beginning by authorizing the Cooperative Research Program. A very few states and local school districts have openly budgeted research and development. Educational foundations have encouraged the use of research in the field as a part of large educational projects. Whether or not educational research, educational experimentation and application of fundamental research from other behavioral research fields can and will be boldly and broadly utilized in education is still not indicated.

Lawrence S. Kubie in a paper entitled *Research in Protecting Preconscious Functions in Education*[3] discusses the many subtle problems of education that must be understood if educational practices are ever to implement the full potential of the learner. Drawing upon the successes and failures in medicine he states the need as he sees it.

> This is precisely what we need in education: research schools to parallel research hospitals. The best schools of tomorrow will be the schools which carry on daily basic research in every detail of the education process, schools with observation chambers and recording equipment, schools with research staffs, schools with at

---

[3] A. Harry Passow, *et al., Nurturing Individual Potential* (Washington, D.C.: Association for Supervision and Curriculum Development, 1964).

least as many professionals as students. There must be research scientists in education working beside the general practitioners of education, just as there are research scientists in medicine working beside the practitioners, each learning from the other. The practitioner reminds the research man of the full complexity of problems as these arise in the classroom and in real life. The investigator reminds the practitioner of the need for more precise methods of observing and of recording and documenting his observations. Each is the conscience of the other: which is why as individuals they sometimes do not get along too well together: they may even fight: but the marriage between them is indissouble.

There will be schools where teachers can sit down with consultants from the fields of child neurology and clinical psychology, cultural anthropology and child psychiatry and child analysis to study films of children alone, and in the classroom, and on the playground, films to give fragmentary samples of episodes in the life of the class as a whole, episodes in the daily life of the group, episodes in the daily lives of special individuals in the group, films which follow the same individual children through years of growth. Such sessions for review and study of what goes on will take time. This is why these schools will need research and teaching staffs several times as large as even the best staffed schools of today enjoy. Yet these sessions for the study of recorded basic data will in the end be as important for each child as are the hours that the teacher today spends marking papers. They will bring the teacher into closer touch with the living spirit of the child. Therefore they will mean at the same time a steady expansion of the spirit of the teacher as well. It is along these lines that I envision studies evolving which can salvage our future in education from enslavement to the past as in medicine and psychiatry.

He further proposes that there should be created a National Institute of Education. Such an institute is needed not only to carry on studies but to link up individuals and agencies for purposes of communication, planning and carrying out related research projects.

The needs are fairly well understood. Principal among these needs are the four following:

Need for an attack on fundamental problems by research institutes, research schools and by individual researchers. The problem here is no different than in any other field of human life. Beginnings have been made in education but they are only beginnings. No clear cut policy exists. Nowhere has a research school been established and equipped with status, money, a multi-disciplinary staff and a mission. Every region or even state in the United States might well have a research school and institute.

Need for institutes of school experimentation designed to work with those in the field on research and development. Here institutions of higher education, special purpose institutes and state departments of education would cooperate with those involved in projects in curriculum development where research findings would be used and the schools and staffs involved would discover new and effective ways of improving teaching and learning.

Need for school service research divisions in all university-type institutions of higher education. Such service divisions should be financed by the institutions, possibly from grants-in-aid, so that they could use the multi-disciplinary staffs of their institutions to support research and development in all field agencies. This concept has been exemplified in agriculture and has had a significant effect. It should work well in education, a field that needs so much research help from so many disciplinary fields.

Such divisions should not be concerned with all types of services such as those that should come from governmental agencies such as departments of education, conservation, health and welfare, but should concentrate on research process and research findings. They should have access to all of the research resources of the institution and especially to research personnel.

Need for acceptance and employment of research and development as a basic part and process of educational administration at the local level. At the heart of the research and development process in a school system would then be curriculum development placed in a proper setting. Subject to attack would be such problems as evaluation of an administrative device such as a principalship, testing instructional materials, analyzing an educational need, developing a program of vocational education, applying a new method in reading or interpreting some new and significant research findings to the total instructional staff. The wide employment of the process of research and development would, it seems, not only bring direct results but would help bring about an acceptance and understanding of behavioral research by the general public since education affects individuals so commonly and so intimately. Educational research and research in health science here have much in common.

Such a process of research and development at the local level would require some highly specialized full-time personnel such as curriculum specialists and researchers. *But, in the main, it would call for a utilization of existing staff in new ways.* Research and educational experimentation at the local level should be centered on the solution of the problems of that locality. Thus research would be carried out by the teachers, specialists, and general administrators of a school system. Emphasis at the local level would always be on local solutions and the extensive use of research findings and consultants.

Implications of research activity. Four implications of a positive solution to the research issue along the lines suggested are so great that they would change the complexion of education. First, if the four needs suggested here were met, the contributions of all agents would fit together and have tremendous impact on education and society. The applications of the finding of fundamental research would be insured. Institutes of school experimentation would have no trouble finding field cooperation. Research people in universities would be in demand and local school systems would be well serviced by research consultants.

Second, the roles of staff specialists involved would be clarified. Teachers could teach creatively, administrators could administer in an inspired fashion, and specialists could serve properly and conspicuously in contributing their specialized skills and unusual knowledge.

Third, the educational foundations, now operating in such an ill-defined relationship to education, would be able to fit into an on-going process having a meaningful organization. Foundation personnel could better analyze the educational situation and decide whether or not to support a certain project.

Fourth, with schools constantly using research as a tool, a process of identification of needed research could be established and servicing institutions could receive a return flow of needed research suggestions to guide them in establishing priorities.

Educational policy on roles of curriculum specialists and related personnel. Issue V—What are the proper roles of curriculum specialists and related personnel?

This problem has been touched upon several times. The issue stands out as an important one. It cannot be settled until the nature of the process of curriculum development, the relationships of the process and the importance of the process are determined. In this sense the five crucial issues are tied together.

The urgency behind arriving at an answer to this issue is great. The public confusion would be greatly reduced if process and role questions were settled. Further, graduate schools are establishing curriculums for the preparation of staff specialists in education.

While they can and will make their own assumptions about role, everyone would be better served if there could be a general consensus on the roles of various kinds of staff specialists and particularly of those who implement the curriculum development process since the situation is so confused as to make the establishment of graduate curriculum very difficult.

The Association for Supervision and Curriculum Development has always had as one of its principal concerns the study of, and definition of, the roles of those members of the education staff giving significant amounts of time to curriculum development. In addition graduate institutions of higher education have been concerned with the problem of defining competencies and specific roles in this field as a basis for developing specialized curriculums in this field. Lawler's study[4] of the factors affecting the success of curriculum consultants represented an indirect approach to the definition of roles and is very helpful.

The first full-scale analysis of the situation appears in the 1956 Yearbook[5] of the Association for Supervision and Curriculum Development. The volume actually deals with the roles of many other curriculum workers than those indicated in the title.

Another report[6] on the same problem defines the situation and the problem rather clearly:

> There is a growing body of specialists whose function it is to support and stimulate teaching and learning. They work at curriculum development, instructional improvement, professional growth, evaluation, and research. They include specialists in guidance, in psychology and child development, in problems of atypical children, in subject areas and special curriculums for adults and the vocations, in health, in in-service growth programs, and in the whole range of instructional materials, media and media services. These persons we call resource people.

> There is no formula for the right number and kinds of resources or resource people in a school system. Each community and each school system has its own needs and priorities. But if education is to be effective most of the resource functions must be performed somewhere in any system. They call for highly specialized compe-

---

[4] Marcella R. Lawler, *Curriculum Consultants at Work* (New York: Bureau of Publications, Teachers College, Columbia University, 1959), Ch. VII.

[5] Association for Supervision and Curriculum Development, *Role of Supervisor and Curriculum Director in a Climate of Change* (Washington, D.C.: The Association, 1965).

[6] American Association of School Administrators and Association for Supervision and Curriculum Development, *Organizing for Improved Instruction* (Washington, D.C.: The Association, 1963), p. 8.

tencies and continuous study which simply cannot be found or maintained in teachers, principals and superintendents who have their own expertness to achieve and hold. No one person could keep abreast of all the specialties.

Every board of education should have a plan for adding resources and resource people which takes into account state requirements and support, community needs and demands and, above all, the needs of the children in its care.

While many authorities state that the principal of the individual school has a major or "the" major role in curriculum leadership, practice presents a very confused picture. There is a great need for (a) an unequivocal agreement on the role of the principal in any given school and (b) a general consensus on the role of the principal as a curriculum leader. Certainly the common practice of making the principal responsible for carrying out plans made by a headquarters echelon is ineffectual and contrary to the philosophy of democratic administration.

The problem of defining roles is complicated in a free society and where vast differences in size and organization of units appear. Thus definition of role in terms of consensuses must be stated in terms of principles. The problem is further complicated by change. The staff of the administrative branch of the Office of Education predicts that the internal administrative staff of school systems will undergo a marked change and that the school principal will assume more responsibility for the instructional program. Research and planning should anticipate these contingencies.[7]

General Implications of the Great Issues

If Issues I and II are settled in such a manner that education will be maximized and decentralized a social role and latitude will be given to curriculum development that should result in appropriate and efficient education. Large needs of society could then be met and an education adjusted to the individual and his way of learning would be highly efficient.

In a society that gives education the central developmental role in regard to the individual, the productivity of the economy and the general nature of the culture, vast changes must be made. A great share of the national effort must be assigned to education. Education must be thought of as an investment rather than a cost.

[7] "Educational Administration in the Decade Ahead," *School Life,* January 1961.

There would develop in such a society a very favorable climate for education which would in turn change the roles of almost every member of society. A youngster would have a firmer feeling about his roles as a learner. Adults in all categories, whether professionalized or not, would seek to carry out roles as both learners and teachers.

If Issues III, IV and V could be settled by positive action on each, the efficient means would exist to keep education up-to-date and effective. Positive action on a policy favorable to curriculum change would give direction to society's agencies for learning and greatly expand the amount of educational activity. The full use of research through educational experimentation and other uses would validate program building and keep education abreast of other developments in a world which is due to change in the foreseeable future with increasing rapidity. Lastly, general agreement on the roles of all people—curriculum specialists, administrators, teachers, research workers, parents and citizens—would open the possibility to much higher levels of educational quality and support than any heretofore experienced.

CHAPTER IX

The Challenging Future of
Curriculum Development

Any person equipped with a reasonable amount of caution and a fairly creative approach to life will address his mind to the contrasting possibilities of cultural collapse and cultural progress. Consideration of the latter will lead inevitably to the nature of a progressive future—to a creative construct based on the potential of education and the employment of the process of curriculum development.

The possibility that man might terminate his history of progress with one great cataclysmic war has never before been so apparent. Social planning and, particularly, diplomacy have taken this possibility into account and built a defense system to cope with known threats to security and progress. Such systems are never perfect and often ineffective. Yet the defense system must be accepted as an insurance policy. Life must go on. Nihilism, anarchism and defeatism build no platforms for future planning.

A reasonable optimism may be based on the quality of international relationships that have developed in the Space Age. The national and international defense mechanisms have given to education its first requirement—a grant of time. This grant of time is given to education just when it is being widely accepted as the primary basis for survival, progress and abundant living in more and more countries throughout the world.

Another important consideration in planning for the future deals with material resources. Thanks to science and a free economy the U.S.A. will be producing goods and services at the rate of two billion dollars a day before the year 1970. Most other economies are showing sharp rises in gross national products. In spite of competition for funds in both private and public sectors, material resources for education become increasingly available. Even in under-developed countries an international program of credits and grants-in-aid makes progress possible.

The technical "know how" which exists in the field of educational research, planning and development is extensive. *It is the process of research and development, at the heart of which lies curriculum development, which gives promise of demonstrating the enlarged role of education in a period of swift social change.* Curriculum development was born out of the social revolution that began with World War I. The planning that went into developing a system of vocational education to supplement apprentice training is a matter of record. The applications of the findings of psychological, physiological and medical research to the field of teaching method are proof that educational progress can result from educational experimentation, careful planning and improved teacher education. The rapid development of new curriculum plans and teaching methods in the field of science education has demonstrated that once social and educational policy concentrates on an educational need resources are unlocked and plans for meeting the need developed.

Time, resources and tested techniques, then, provide adequate bases for educational and social process since one depends so much on the other.

It is too much to say that the large process of research and development has justified itself in the field of education—but the promise is there. The present rate of innovation and improvement in education scarcely equals the rate of social change—it scarcely helps society to keep up. Consequently some way of speeding up invention and dissemination of results must be accepted if progress is to be achieved. Probably the answer lies in magnification of research and development processes that are already explored. A superimposed method of curriculum reform that does not avail itself of existing processes defies the political forces involved in educational change. It also ignores the local or community influences affecting education as well as the power of a profession to resist aggression and also to lead a curriculum reform movement once the profession has become convinced of the need for curriculum change.

The Vistas of the Future

The future, at its optimistic best, holds a promise of a world engrossed in education as a means to a finer way of life. This education must be democratic in nature and must take place in a framework of democratic administration. This can be assumed because only in a democratic society can education be democratic in both means and ends.

The investment in research and development must be substantial to guarantee the main investment in education which will be about ten per cent of the gross national product on the average. Traditional packages of teaching-learning process will be subjected to severe tests of authenticity and effectiveness. In each area the process of invention will be employed. Through creative curriculum development teams of specialists and creative teachers will invent new teaching-learning processes and test them through action research and objective evaluation. The equipment and materials of instruction will be subjected to scientific tests. *A priori* assumptions about teaching machines and aids of various kinds will serve only as points of departure. Industry will be encouraged to use all of its efforts to invent and produce new materials and equipment.

The chief role science will play, however, will be in the study of the human being and his conditions, needs and nature. The findings of the behavioral sciences translated into creative methods of teaching and therapy will assure progress.

Universalizing good practices.   The failure to utilize best practices in education is well known. In the U.S.A. every survey tells the story. In a world-wide sense the problem is more acute because of gaps in communication, language barriers and nationalism that are often as impenetrable as parochialism. A recent report[1] of the Association for Supervision and Curriculum Development illustrates the failure in a dramatic manner. On the same day observations were taken in 98 junior high schools in 26 states. The findings showed almost no evidence of the careful application of tested practices although the quality of teaching observed left much room for application and invention.

Probably the tendency of research and development to concentrate on invention rather than widespread application or universalization has been desirable during the early formative years of curriculum development. It was very necessary to invent a program of educational excursions, to explore the possibilities of audio-visual education, to put a language laboratory together for the first time and to try it out. The challenge of the future is to continue to invent but *also* to mount vigorous programs of widespread application. Universalization of the use of techniques seems imperative in a space age. In surgery, the language barriers are being surmounted and new

---

[1] John H. Lounsbury and Jean Marani, *The Junior High School We Saw,* (Washington, D.C.: Association for Supervision and Curriculum Development, 1964).

techniques are reported quite promptly and quite promptly applied by the diplomats of the profession. This has never been true in education but universalization of techniques, not curriculums, now seems practical.

The need for universalization of the techniques of meeting educational needs on the world scene is illustrated by the dramatic attempts of the U.S.S.R. to meet the needs of its political philosophy and social plan. The need is even more dramatically illustrated by the numerous countries just emerging from colonialism which are seeking literacy and technical education as they try to free themselves from obsolete European or Asiatic patterns and practices. Imagine the task facing Nigeria, Algeria, Brazil, India or Korea to say nothing of dozens of smaller countries such as Somalia and Nepal.

Progress Depends on Many Factors

Any assumption that any country, whether highly developed or poorly developed, could put its education in order either quantitatively or qualitatively in a short time such as a decade or two would be unfounded. The need for new research, the need for new researchers, the need for re-educated teachers, the need for personnel to prepare such teachers, the need for curriculum specialists, the need for personnel to prepare such specialists—all of these needs must be met sequentially to guarantee progress.

While the U.S.A. has a large group of fairly well prepared and well experienced curriculum specialists, this group would meet only a small part of the need if curriculum development were to be taken seriously by every school district and educational authority in the country. To expand the supply and to bring about the kind of specialist that will be needed in the future would take much unlocking of resources, redesigning of graduate programs, recruiting of candidates suitable for scholarships and restaffing of graduate departments. The same needs would hold to some degree in preparing enough educational administrators, researchers and other key personnel. Besides meeting their own needs highly developed countries must be prepared to loan a large number of specialists to the international aid program of the future.

Extensive research and development programs. The role of research and development has been discussed. The future should bring about its implementation. *Either education will fail in its mission or research and its application will predominate.* This means that the logic of the future points definitely to an emphasis on research and development. By 1950 it was apparent that the allocation of from two to five per cent of an educational budget to evaluation and improvement was totally inadequate. With a better perception of the need for program change, with an increase in social change and scientific invention and with better techniques of research and program planning available, research and program development should occupy nearly all of the time of creative administrators and staff specialists. Routine administrative work can be made largely automatic. Teachers will need to be involved more. Thus from ten to fifteen per cent of an educational budget might be spent wisely on research and development, broadly interpreted. Such a budget would provide for staff, for supplies, for equipment, for materials and materials development, for research and application of research findings, for financing staff growth programs including scholarships, released time for teachers, action research projects, formal in-service education and on-the-job guidance of teachers.

The role of the extra-community agencies has been indicated in a general way. As of now the role of state and national governments is not too clear. The Congress of the U.S.A. has entered the field with several projects. India has set up a novel institution at the national level called the National Council for Educational Research and Training. Possibly institutionalization of this kind rather than that represented by a simple legislative act may be the method of the future. Undoubtedly each state and country will find its own solution but it seems certain that the focus will not be on inquiry for inquiry's sake—or on erudition as such but rather on swift and pragmatic curriculum development to meet needs such as vocational proficiency in a semi-primitive culture, international understanding for all peoples or supplying scientists capable of unravelling the secrets of social relationships, biological phenomena and physical forces.

Overt recognition of international-intercultural relationships.[2] Since World War II and the advent of the United Nations, the Marshall Plan, the Fulbright Scholarships, the Point Four Program and more recently the Agency for International Development, there has been a tacit understanding that under certain conditions the government of the United States would provide technical assistance to other countries. Private agencies preceded the government in this

---

[2] *See* C. E. Speakman, Jr., *International Exchange in Education* (New York: The Center for Applied Research in Education, Inc., 1966) for further discussion of international-intercultural exchange.

policy and continue to provide technical assistance. The policies and ground rules are complicated and often very specious. As yet there is no international curriculum development rationale or policy. The United Nations has no broad program in this field although the United Nations Educational, Scientific and Cultural Organization has made some contributions to curriculum development. There is no professional agency concerned with curriculum development that is international in scope. There is no consensus on the relation of curriculum, as such, or curriculum development, as a process, to national development on the one hand and good international intercultural relations on the other. Nor are these one and the same thing.

On the positive side it can be said only that there exists a general belief that education is good for the individual and society and that a high priority should be placed on literacy and the production of technicians.

The present situation, while indeterminate, suggests that the time may be ripe for the development of a broad program of cooperation between countries, using the ideas and technicians now available. This approach would be both governmental and non-governmental. The important element would be the utilization of knowledgeable and skillful people in all countries. Technical cooperation as developed at the university level and described in the recent study released by the U.S. Government[3] would be one essential aspect of the program. The main purpose would be the development of programs at the public school level. It can now be seen that programs should represent a broader approach than literacy or an attack on analphabetism as needful as that may be. It should deal more with general education and citizenship education. It should be as modern as is modern technology and as advanced as is space science.

If such a program is to come it must come either by fiat in an autocratic state and thus be "bare bones" or it must come through the very democratic, multi-disciplinary process of curriculum development. If it comes by the slow, democratic route it will have a difficult time and tardy acceptance at the hands of the ruling elders but it will have the flexibility and tenacity to prove itself and to improve itself.

The importance of intercultural by-products.   Should curriculum development break out onto the world stage it would have the obvious benefits previously referred to. Furthermore, curriculum

---

[3] John W. Gardner, *A.I.D. and the Universities,* (Washington, D.C.: Agency for International Development, 1964).

development would have so many important by-products that their value would seem to be almost equal to the central product of more and better education. Should all countries seek to provide education of a democratic nature developed by a democratic process, democracy itself would be enhanced. Secondly, widespread curriculum development would bring people together in a world-wide effort to employ and improve a generative process. A joint effort by people of all stations of life and all countries would be tremendously important from an intercultural point of view.

Thirdly, the development of an educational program by a multidisciplinary process would utilize all disciplines and cause representatives of all disciplines to deal with the "explosion of knowledge" or, in other words, the increased and much more diversified educational needs of people in a space age.

Lastly, curriculum development, dealing as it does with all educational needs, would develop programs carefully adjusted to individuals. The nature of individuals would be considered in meeting society's demands on education. Technicians in the field of therapy, sociology and philosophy would collaborate with physicists, chemists, linguists and mathematicians in developing balanced programs of education. For what is good for the individual is good for society and vice versa. Curriculum development is concerned with mediating apparent conflicts and developing a socially desirable kind of education.

In conclusion it can be said a new air of confidence has swept into the nation's educational program. The strides have been gigantic although the remaining unsolved problems are still prodigious.

Bibliography

Alberty, Harold, *Reorganizing the High School Curriculum* (New York: The Macmillan Company, 1953).

American Association of School Administrators, National Education Association, *Imperatives in Education* (Washington, D.C.: The Association, 1966).

————, ————, *The Federal Government and Public Schools* (Washington, D.C.: The Association, 1965).

Association for Supervision and Curriculum Development, National Education Association, *Individualizing Instruction,* 1964 Yearbook (Washington, D.C.: The Association, 1964).

————, ————, *New Curriculum Developments* (Washington, D.C.: The Association, 1965).

————, ————, *Nurturing Individual Potential* (Washington, D.C.: The Association, 1964).

————, ————, *Role of Supervisor and Curriculum Director in a Climate of Change* (Washington, D.C.: The Association, 1965).

————, ————, *The Elementary School We Need* (Washington, D.C.: The Association, 1965).

————, ————, *The High School We Need* (Washington, D.C.: The Association, 1959).

————, ————, *The Junior High School We Need* (Washington, D.C.: The Association, 1961).

————, ————, *Theories of Instruction* (Washington, D.C.: The Association, 1965).

Bobbitt, Franklin, *The Curriculum of Modern Education* (New York: McGraw-Hill Book Company, 1941).

Campbell, Roald F., and Robert A. Bunnell, eds., *Nationalizing Influences on Secondary Education* (Chicago: University of Chicago, Midwest Administration Center, 1963).

Caswell, Hollis L., and Doak S. Campbell, eds., *Readings in Curriculum Development* (New York: American Book Company, 1937).

Dewey, John, *How We Think* (Boston: D. C. Heath and Company, 1933).

Everett, Samuel, ed., *A Challenge to Secondary Education* (New York: Appleton-Century-Crofts, 1935).

————, *The Community School* (New York: Appleton-Century-Crofts, Inc., 1938).

Faunce, Roland C., and Nelson L. Bossing, *Developing the Core Curriculum* (Englewood Cliffs, N.J.: Prentice-Hall, Inc., 1951).

Frankel, M. L., *Economic Education* (New York: The Center for Applied Research in Education, Inc., 1965).

Goodlad, John I., *School Curriculum Reform in the United States* (New York: The Fund for the Advancement of Education, March 1964).

Kelley, Earl C., *The Workshop Way of Learning* (New York: Harper & Row, Publishers, 1951).

Kenworthy, Leonard S., *World Horizons for Teachers* (New York: Bureau of Publications, Teachers College, Columbia University, 1952).

Koopman, G. Robert, Alice Miel, and Paul Misner, *Democracy in School Administration* (New York: Appleton-Century-Crofts, Inc., 1943).

Long, Harold M., and Robert N. King, *Improving the Teaching of World Affairs—The Glens Falls Story* (Washington, D.C.: National Council for the Social Studies, National Education Association, 1964).

Lawler, Marcella R., *Curriculum Consultants at Work* (New York: Bureau of Publications, Teachers College, Columbia University, 1958).

McKean, Robert C., and H. H. Mills, *The Supervisor* (New York: The Center for Applied Research in Education, Inc., 1964).

Melby, Ernest O., *The Teacher and Learning* (New York: The Center for Applied Research in Education, Inc., 1963).

Alice Miel, *et al.*, *Cooperative Procedures in Learning* (New York: Bureau of Publications, Teachers College, Columbia University, 1952).

National Society for the Study of Education, *Curriculum Making: Past and Present*, 26th Yearbook Part I (Bloomington, Ill.: Public School Publishing Co., 1926).

Neill, A. S., *Summerhill* (New York: Hart Publishing Company, 1960).

Olson, Willard C., *Child Development* (Boston: D. C. Heath Company, 1949).

Parrish, Louise, and Yvonne Waskin, *Teacher-Pupil Planning—For Better Curriculum Learning* (New York: Harper & Row, Publishers, 1958).

Rickover, H. G., *Education and Freedom* (New York: E. P. Dutton and Co., 1959).

Reisner, Edward H., *Nationalism and Education Since 1789* (New York: The Macmillan Company, 1922).

Rugg, Harold, ed., *Democracy and the Curriculum* (New York: Appleton-Century-Crofts, Inc., 1939).

Saylor, J. Galen, and William M. Alexander, *Curriculum Planning for Better Teaching and Learning* (New York: Holt, Rinehart, & Winston, Inc., 1954).

Tuttle, Edward M., *School Board Leadership in America,* rev. ed. (Danville, Ill.: The Interstate Printers and Publishers, 1963).

U.S. Department of Health, Education, and Welfare, Office of Education, *Progress of Public Education in the United States of America, 1960–61* (Washington, D.C.: U.S. Government Printing Office, 1961).

————, *Programs for the Educationally Disadvantaged* (Washington, D.C.: U.S. Government Printing Office, 1963).

Weber, C. A., and Mary E. Weber, *Fundamentals of Educational Leadership* (New York: McGraw-Hill Book Co., 1955).

Zirbes, Laura, *Spurs to Creative Teaching* (New York: G. P. Putnam's Sons, 1959).

Index